5,000 MILES TO FREEDOM

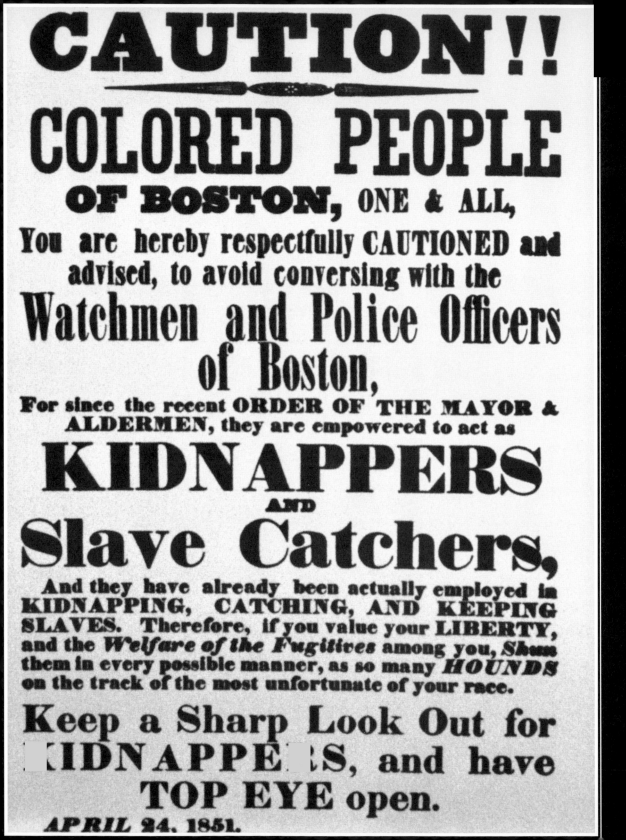

5,000 MILES TO FREEDOM

Ellen and William Craft's Flight from Slavery

BY JUDITH BLOOM FRADIN
AND
DENNIS BRINDELL FRADIN

NATIONAL GEOGRAPHIC
WASHINGTON, D.C.

◎ AUTHORS' NOTE ◎

The following story is true. Old documents, letters, diaries, newspapers, speeches, and personal narratives provided most of the information for this book. Running a Thousand Miles for Freedom, *by William and Ellen Craft, is the source for nearly all of the dialogue. Please see the notes and bibliography at the back of the book for further details.*

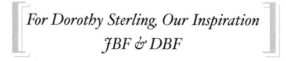

For Dorothy Sterling, Our Inspiration
JBF & DBF

Text copyright © 2006 Judith Bloom Fradin and Dennis Brindell Fradin
Maps copyright © 2006 National Geographic Society

Published by the National Geographic Society.
All rights reserved. Reproduction of the whole or any part of the contents without written permission
from the National Geographic Society is strictly prohibited.

Book design by Bea Jackson, Ruthie Thompson, and David M. Seager
The body text of the book is set in Hoefler New Roman.
The display text is set in Ferao, Dekora, and Steelplate Gothic Shaded.

Library of Congress Cataloging-in-Publication Data is available
from the Library of Congress

Hardcover ISBN: 0-7922-7885-2
Library Edition ISBN: 0-7922-7886-0

Printed in the U.S.A.

Illustration credits: Aldridge family: p. 91; Boston Public Library: p. 46; Central of Georgia Railway Historical Society:
p. 24; Corbis: p. 19, 50, 52, 64; Courtesy of Herbert and Emily DeCosta: p. 68, 69; Courtesy Georgia Division of Archives
and History, Office of Secretary of State: p. 28; Illustrated London News: p. 66; Library of Congress: pp. 2, 6, 8, 16, 20, 26,
35, 36, 76, 77, 78, 83; Courtesy of Mississippi Department of Archives and History: p. 80; North Wind Picture Archives:
pp. 10, 31, 40, 43 masthead, 60; Northwestern University Library Special Collections Department: p. 73;
Picturehistory.com: p. 13; Pat Pflieger Collection: p. 45; Virginia Craft Rose: p. 88

One of the world's largest nonprofit scientific and educational organizations, the National Geographic Society was founded
in 1888 "for the increase and diffusion of geographic knowledge." Fulfilling this mission, the Society educates and inspires millions
every day through its magazines, books, television programs, videos, maps and atlases, research grants, the National Geographic Bee,
teacher workshops, and innovative classroom materials. The Society is supported through membership dues, charitable gifts,
and income from the sale of its educational products. This support is vital to National Geographic's mission to increase
global understanding and promote conservation of our planet through exploration, research, and education.

For more information, please call 1-800-NGS-LINE (647-5463) or write to the following address:

NATIONAL GEOGRAPHIC SOCIETY
1145 17th Street N.W.
Washington, D.C. 20036-4688
U.S.A.

Visit the Society's Web site: www.nationalgeographic.com

CHAPTER ONE

A DESPERATE LEAP
FOR
LIBERTY

Stars still twinkled over their cabin as Ellen and William Craft awoke on the morning of December 21, 1848. The shivering couple climbed out of bed and lit a candle. Neither the chill air nor the early hour dampened their spirits, for the moment they had dreamed about had arrived.

Anyone peeking through the Crafts' window on that first day of winter would have seen a strange sight. First, William found a scissors. As his wife bowed her head, he snipped away until most of her hair lay on the cabin floor. Next, the couple unlocked a chest of drawers where they had hidden an elegant set of men's clothing. But Ellen, not William, dressed in these garments.

Ellen stepped into the trousers and buttoned the white shirt. With William's help, she attached the necktie and pulled on the high-heeled boots. To cover her pretty eyes, Ellen donned a pair of green-tinted spectacles. To hide her smooth cheeks and chin, she tied a handkerchief around her face, as people suffering from toothaches often did. William placed a bandage and sling over Ellen's right arm, as if she had arthritis. Ellen then slipped into the black jacket and the cloak. After William placed the top hat upon his wife's head to complete her costume, Ellen stood before him with a look of uncertainty on her face.

"You make a most respectable-looking gentleman," William reassured her. He dressed in his usual work clothes that morning, adding just one special item: a fancy beaver hat.

*Slave quarters on a Southern plantation, Ellen and William's cabin
may have been similar to these.*

Slaves were at the mercy of their owners, and captured runaways were punished ruthlessly, sometimes even killed.

The couple's future—perhaps their lives—would depend upon the success or failure of their masquerade. The Crafts were slaves in Macon, Georgia. Over the next few days they hoped to travel one thousand miles to Philadelphia, Pennsylvania, where they would be free. Ellen, a light-skinned African American, was pretending to be "Mr. William Johnson," a wealthy white Southern gentleman heading north to Philadelphia to consult a physician for a variety of ailments. William, who was dark skinned, was posing as Mr. Johnson's slave.

Their chances of reaching free soil were slim, they knew. The risks were enormous. If captured, they could expect to be sold apart, never to see one another again. They might also be tortured for having run away. William and Ellen had heard of runaways who were branded with red-hot irons and whipped almost to the point of death. Georgia slave owners also used the picket, a fiendish torture in which slaves were tied to scaffolds and lowered toward sharp stakes sticking out of the ground. The stakes punctured their feet, sometimes leaving the slaves crippled. But despite the risks, Ellen and William Craft were determined to gain their liberty— or die trying.

As the stars began to fade from the sky, the couple knew it was time to depart. They blew out the candle, knelt down, and prayed for deliverance from bondage. When they arose, William raised the latch and glanced outside. Nothing was stirring except the pine trees swaying in the early-morning breeze.

"Come, my dear," William whispered, "let us make a desperate leap for liberty!"

Standing by the cabin door, Ellen suddenly felt that their scheme was hopeless and that her costume wouldn't fool anyone. Tears filled her eyes as she clasped her husband tightly. Ellen gathered her courage. "It is getting late, William," she said, "so let us begin our journey."

Once outside, they headed off, taking separate routes toward the Macon train station. Ellen's route took her past the estate where her mother, Maria, lived along the Ocmulgee River. She yearned to stop and say good-bye but knew she couldn't. If Maria learned of Ellen and William's escape, she might be tortured to make her reveal her daughter's plan.

William reached the station first and stowed their suitcase in the baggage compartment of a waiting Georgia Central train. He boarded the "Negro car," in which black passengers were required to ride, and pulled his hat down to hide his face. Ellen arrived at the station a short time later. So nervous that she could barely speak, she walked up to the ticket window and purchased tickets for William Johnson and slave to travel to Savannah, Georgia, some 200 miles away. Ellen then boarded one of the whites-only train cars and sat down, relieved that, so far, no one had questioned Mr. Johnson's identity.

CHAPTER TWO

YEARS in BONDAGE

When Ellen and William Craft set off on their "desperate leap for liberty" in 1848, the United States was 72 years old. The nation had changed in important ways since the Declaration of Independence had been issued in Philadelphia in 1776.

Transportation had been revolutionized. The first commercially successful steamboats had been built in the early 1800s. By mid-century, steamboats were traveling rivers in many parts of the country, while larger vessels called "steamships" were carrying people and cargo overseas. In 1829, Englishman George Stephenson created the first successful train locomotive, which traveled at the then mind-boggling speed of about 30 miles per hour. By the 1840s, railroads were chugging back and forth between hundreds of American towns. For example, the Georgia Central Railroad on which the Crafts began their journey had completed its line between Macon and Savannah five years earlier in 1843. Besides passengers, the Georgia Central transported large quantities of cotton to market, boosting Georgia's cotton-growing industry.

Steamboats and trains made long-distance travel much faster and easier than it had ever been before. Back in 1776, the trip between Georgia and Pennsylvania could take weeks. By 1848, the journey between the two states could be made by train and steamboat in just four days.

A young house slave fans her master and his guests; house slaves cleaned, cooked, and sewed for their owners.

Communication had also been revolutionized since our nation's birth. In 1844 American inventor Samuel F. B. Morse sent the first telegraph message. The telegraph, which was the first apparatus to send messages electrically, enabled people to communicate by using special codes. Within a few years, the country was connected by a network of telegraph lines. Instead of being limited to handwritten letters that might take weeks to arrive, people could communicate over long distances almost instantly. So important was the new invention that a Macon newspaper adopted the name the *Georgia Telegraph*.

Of course, the United States of 1848 differed in many ways from the nation we know today. There were no electric lights as yet. Light was provided by oil and gas lamps and by candles. Radio, TV, and movies had not been invented. For entertainment, people attended lectures, plays, and concerts. There were no typewriters or computers. Children and adults wrote out lessons, letters, and other documents by hand. With no telephones, people spent much more time visiting friends and relatives than they do today. Americans in the 1840s lived to an average age of only about 40 compared to about 77 today. Doctors did not yet know that germs cause disease, and there were no antibiotics.

Instead of 50, the nation had only 30 states in 1848, with Wisconsin having been admitted as the newest state that May. Today the nation has nearly 300 million people, but back in 1848 it had less than a tenth that total: about 22 million. But perhaps the biggest difference was that, in the 1840s, the southern states allowed slavery. Approximately three million black Southerners—roughly a seventh of the country's entire population—were slaves as of 1848. In portions of the South, the slaves were as numerous as the whites. Bibb County, Georgia, where Macon was located, was home to roughly 7,000 whites and 5,600 black slaves.

Slaves did most of the work in the South. The majority of them were field slaves. They grew the cotton, rice, and tobacco that southern planters depended on for their livelihood. Slave children as young as seven or eight worked in the fields, sometimes up to 16 hours a day. Field slaves were housed in small log huts. They were dressed in skimpy clothing, fed moldy corn and bacon, and whipped when they fell behind in their work.

Even young children were forced to work long days in the cotton fields of the South. Ellen and William were considered lucky to avoid such hard physical labor.

· —— ·

Other black Southerners were house slaves. They did the cooking, cleaning, and much of the child raising for their owners. The house slaves were the envy of the field slaves, for they were often allowed to live in the owners' "big house," wear their cast-off clothing, and eat their leftovers.

A few slaves with special skills worked as blacksmiths, dressmakers, hairdressers, bricklayers, or carpenters. These skilled workers were allowed to leave their owners' property and work at jobs in town. Most of their pay went to their owners, but typically they were permitted to keep a small portion of their earnings with which to buy clothing or food for their families.

Whether they worked in the fields, in the big house, or in town as laborers, slaves had certain things in common. First and foremost, they were considered property, with no more rights than a horse or cow. Slaves generally didn't even have their own last names, but were called by their owners' surnames. Masters who needed money often sold their slaves, separating parents and children in the process. If a master liked the looks of a female slave, he was free to enter her cabin and force himself on her, for there was no such crime as rape of a slave by an owner. Since children born of slave women were automatically slaves from birth, and therefore valuable property, masters who fathered children by their female slaves increased their wealth. Any slave who raised a hand against his or her owner could be put to death, with the master suffering no more legal trouble than had he killed a rabid dog.

Although killing slaves was legal, any white person caught teaching a slave to read and write faced being fined and jailed. Educated slaves might read the Declaration of Independence, which asserts that "all men are created equal" and entitled to "Life, Liberty, and the pursuit of Happiness." Worse yet, as far as their owners were concerned, literate slaves might pass notes to one another and plan what white Southerners feared most: a slave revolt.

Thirteen years earlier, in 1835, there had been talk of an impending slave revolt in Monroe County, Georgia, near Macon. Rumors had circulated that on election day, when the white men would be voting and drinking the alcohol that office-seekers freely handed out, the slaves would make a surprise attack. Before this plot could be carried out, a slave named George was identified as the main ringleader. Back in Revolutionary days, Patrick Henry had been hailed as a great patriot for saying, "Give me liberty or give me death!"

But for seeking *his* liberty, George was hanged. An alleged accomplice was branded and whipped and had his ears partially cut off.

Such revolts were rare, but thousands of slaves ran away. Many of the country's 425,000 free black people as of 1848 were former slaves who had escaped or descendants of runaway slaves. To make escape difficult, slaves were required to carry written passes when away from home. Any white person could demand to see this pass, and a slave who couldn't produce it risked arrest. In areas with a large slave population, heavily-armed groups of white men took turns patrolling their neighborhoods in search of runaways. When a slave was known to have run away, a mob gathered for what was called a "nigger hunt." Following the North Star at night, a small percentage of fugitive slaves escaped to freedom in the Northern states, which did not

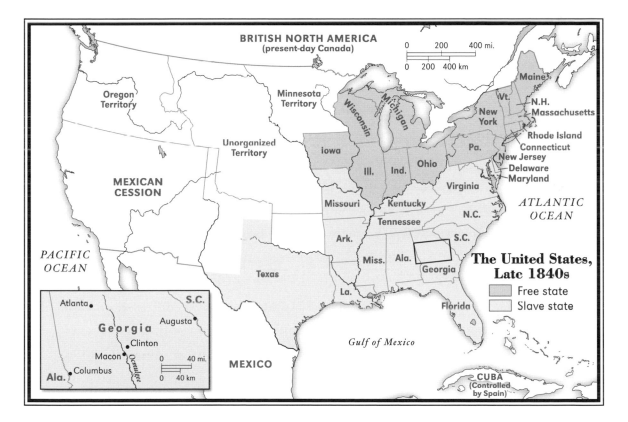

The United States was deeply divided on the subject of slavery.
The Southern states allowed it, and the Northern states forbade it. Because
the country was so evenly divided, each time a state joined the Union a
struggle broke out over whether it would be slave or free.

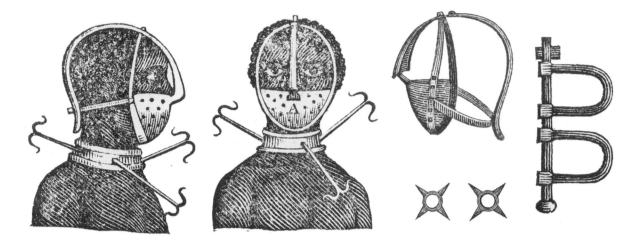

Instruments of torture such as these were used to punish slaves and restrict their movement.

allow slavery. Most, however, were unable to get past the mountains, woods, and rivers that blocked their path to freedom. Captured runaways were brought back in chains and subjected to the cruelest tortures their owners could devise.

Slavery was a subject of bitter dispute among Americans in the 1840s. Originally, all 13 American colonies had allowed slavery. Only after independence was declared in 1776 did some states begin to outlaw the evil practice. By 1848 the nation was evenly split, with 15 states (often called "the North" or the "Free States") having outlawed slavery and another 15 (called "the South" or the "Slave States") still permitting it.

Many white people in the North, and some in the South, wanted to end slavery throughout the country. Because of their desire to get rid of, or *abolish,* slavery, they were called "abolitionists." Hundreds of abolitionists turned their homes into stops on the Underground Railroad—a series of hiding places where escaped slaves were sheltered and fed on their northward journey to the Free States. But nearly all of the slaves who escaped to free soil came from states near the North such as Maryland, Virginia, and Kentucky. Rarely did a slave accomplish what the Crafts were attempting: to travel a thousand miles from the Deep South state of Georgia, which, until Florida joined the Union in 1845, had been the state in the nation's southeast corner.

When they boarded the Georgia Central train four days before Christmas in 1848, Ellen and William Craft were 22 and 25 years old, respectively. Both of them had spent their entire lives as slaves.

Ellen had been born in 1826 in the little town of Clinton in central Georgia. Her father, Major James Smith, was a wealthy white man who owned a hotel and plantation in Clinton, vast tracts of land around the state, and approximately one hundred slaves. Among those slaves was a young woman named Maria, who cooked, cleaned, and helped care for Major and Mrs. Smith's children. Major Smith found Maria attractive and broke into her cabin at night. When 17-year-old Maria became pregnant, the major was pleased. He would be not only the father but also the owner of Maria's baby.

The child born of the union of Maria the house slave and Major James Smith was named Ellen. The little girl was very close to her mother, as they sewed, cooked, washed clothes, and did other household work together.

Serving as her own father's slave hurt the little girl, but the treatment she received at Mrs. Smith's hands was even worse. No matter how carefully Ellen dusted the furniture or washed the floors, the major's wife found something wrong and yelled at her or slapped her. The worst times were when guests came to the Smith plantation. Because Ellen was light-skinned and resembled her father, visitors often assumed she was Major and Mrs. Smith's daughter. They even told Mrs. Smith that Ellen was the prettiest of their children. Mrs. Smith would turn red and explain that Ellen was her *slave,* not her daughter. After their guests left, Mrs. Smith would go into a rage and whip Ellen. The girl was too young to understand that Mrs. Smith resented her because she was a constant reminder of the major's infidelity.

Maria could only comfort her daughter with hugs and soothing words. Weren't they much better off than the field slaves? Didn't they get to eat the Smiths' leftovers and wear their hand-me-down clothes? Didn't they get to work in their owners' mansion instead of out in the cotton fields?

When Ellen was 11 years old, Mrs. Smith finally found a way to get rid of her. The Smiths' 18-year-old daughter Eliza was about to marry Dr. Robert Collins, a prominent resident of Macon, a young town 12 miles from Clinton in the heart of a great cotton-growing region. Mrs. Smith decided to give Ellen to her daughter as a wedding present.

Miss Eliza Smith married Dr. Robert Collins in April 1837. When the newlyweds left for Macon, Ellen was dragged from her mother and forced to enter the carriage with them. She was taken to Macon, where she was put to work as her half-sister Eliza's personal maid.

Like a real-life Cinderella, Ellen had to obey her half-sister's orders. She cooked, cleaned, and sewed for Eliza and Dr. Collins, just like her mother continued to do for the Smiths back in Clinton. Whenever guests visited the Collins mansion, Ellen served them. Although the two of them had the same father, Ellen had to call Eliza "Ma'am" and refer to her as "my mistress."

William's early life had been more difficult than Ellen's. Born in Georgia in 1823, he came from a large and loving family that worked in the cotton fields. But one day their owner, Mr. Craft, stopped by their cabin and led William's parents away. "They are getting old," he explained, and he was determined to sell them while they still had some value. William's parents were sold to different owners, never to see one another again.

The loss of their parents was a crushing blow to William and his two brothers and two sisters, but at least they still had each other. That soon changed. Needing more money, Mr. Craft sold both of William's brothers and one of his sisters. Now only William and his sister Sarah remained together. However, Mr. Craft wanted to invest in cotton, so he took out a bank loan, offering William and Sarah as security. This meant that if Mr. Craft couldn't repay the loan, William and Sarah would become the bank's property. As it turned out, Mr. Craft did fail to make his loan payments. The bank then took possession of 16-year-old William and his 14-year-old sister and sent them to the slave market to be sold to the highest bidder.

Sarah was placed on the auction block first. William watched in anguish as white men examined his sister's teeth and felt her muscles to determine her value. A planter who lived far out in the country placed the highest bid on Sarah and prepared to take her away in a cart.

This might be his last chance to be with his sister, William realized. Desperate to say farewell to her, he pleaded with the man who had bought Sarah to wait a few minutes before departing. But Sarah's new owner said he had a long way to go and refused to wait.

Falling to his knees, William begged the auctioneer to let him step down from the platform to say good-bye to his sister. The auctioneer seized him by his neck and commanded: "Get up! You can do the wench no good!" When William stood, he saw Sarah staring back at him with tears streaming down her cheeks. This image of the last member of his family being hauled away in a cart haunted William for the rest of his life.

William remained in a daze as the bidding for him began. He was bought by Mr. Ira Taylor, a cashier at the bank that had seized ownership of William and Sarah.

A short time before he had been forced to give William up, Mr. Craft had removed him from the cotton fields and sent him into Macon to work in a cabinet shop. Mr. Taylor ordered William to return to work at this establishment. Although most of his salary from making cabinets went to Mr. Taylor, William was allowed to keep some of it. He also worked a second job. Across the street from the cabinet shop was a hotel, which hired William to wait

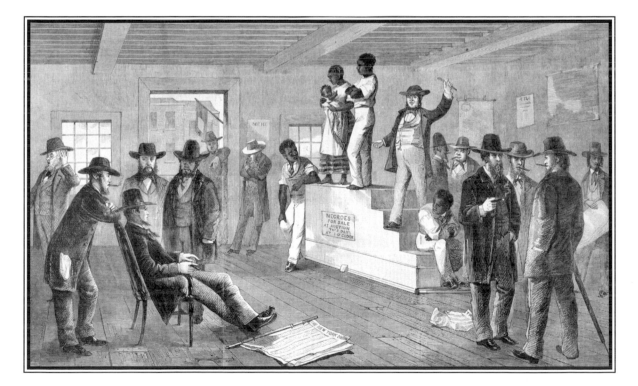

Slaves were treated as property, not as people.
The members of this family could be sold to separate buyers.

> (BILL OF SALE.)
>
> Printed and Sold by J. ROBINSON, Circulating Library, No. 110 Baltimore-street,—*Baltimore.*
>
> **KNOW ALL MEN BY THESE PRESENTS,** That *I John Barnett of Talbot County* and State of Maryland, for and in consideration of the sum of *fifty dollars* lawful money of the United States in hand paid by *Washington Limberry of the City of Baltimore and State of Maryland* at or before the sealing and delivery of these presents, the receipt whereof is hereby acknowledged **HAVE** granted, bargained and sold, and by these presents **DO** grant, bargain and sell, unto the said *Washington Limberry* ~~his Executors, Administrators and Assigns~~ *One negro girl named Georgiana about three years old, to serve the said Washington Limberry untill she arrives at the age of Sixteen years, and then to be free from Servitude to any one, That is to say she shall be free on the first day of January in the year 1856 —*

This receipt records the sale of a three-year-old slave girl named Georgiana. Washington Limberry bought her for $50, about $1,000 in today's money.

tables at night in exchange for a room in which he could sleep. William probably worked 100 hours a week, making a great deal of money for Mr. Taylor and enjoying a large measure of freedom for a slave.

Ellen, meanwhile, had shown a talent for sewing. She did the sewing for the Collinses and their children, and earned extra money for her owners by making clothing for other people in Macon. Her half-sister and Dr. Collins rewarded Ellen by permitting her to move into a small cabin in the woods behind their mansion. By this time, Ellen's former owners, the Smiths, had moved with their house slaves to Macon, too. For Ellen this was great news because it meant she could see her mother again. On Sundays, Ellen and Maria were given passes and allowed to go on walks around town together.

When William was around 21 and Ellen about 18 years old, their paths crossed in Macon. Perhaps Ellen was sent on an errand to the cabinet shop where William worked, or they may have met on the street during one of Ellen and Maria's Sunday walks. Ellen and William fell in love. Slaves weren't allowed to have official marriage ceremonies, so William and Ellen had a "slave wedding." They said they were husband and wife in front of friends, and William moved into Ellen's cabin on the Collins estate. The Collinses were pleased because any children the couple had would be their property.

Ellen and William couldn't bear the thought of having their as-yet-unborn children owned by other people and, even worse, taken from them and sold. They decided to remain childless as long as they were slaves, which they hoped would not be for long.

❧⚡❧

**Ellen and William couldn't bear
the thought of having
their as-yet-unborn children
owned by other people and, even worse,
taken from them and sold.**

❧⚡❧

Occasionally, while waiting tables at the hotel, William overheard white people complain about slaves who had escaped to the Free States or to Canada. That country north of the United States had outlawed slavery in 1834. Now and then, while serving guests at the Collins mansion, Ellen heard talk about the "damned abolitionists" or "that damned Underground Railroad." These topics had to do with slave escapes, Ellen realized, but the white people spoke with such venom that she actually believed the abolitionists were monsters and the Underground Railroad was a place in Hell.

At night in their cabin, the couple whispered about something that would have infuriated their owners: escaping to the North. This idea seemed more like a dream than something that could actually happen, though, for how could they cross a thousand miles of woods, mountains, and alligator-infested swamps?

Then, in December of 1848, an odd plan popped into William's head. Having been raised among white people, Ellen spoke like a white Southern lady. If Ellen impersonated a white man, and William pretended to be her— or rather "his"— slave, they could try to escape to the North by train and steamboat.

· — ·

This idea might have been inspired by an incident in Ellen's family. Years earlier, Ellen's cousins Frank and Mary had escaped from slavery pretending to be a white couple. Disguised as a white man, Frank had later returned and rescued his and Mary's younger sister and brother from slavery.

When William first told his wife about his idea, she laughed. But when she realized that he was serious, she was horrified. The chances seemed overwhelming that somewhere along the thousand-mile journey they would be discovered and captured. Then they might be tortured or sold to separate

How would they convince the people
at the Macon train station,
let alone the hundreds of white people
they would meet along the way,
that Ellen was a white man?

owners, never to see one another again.

Ellen pointed out one obstacle after another. How would they convince people at the Macon train station, let alone the hundreds of white people they would meet along the way, that Ellen was a white man? Since they couldn't read or write, what would Ellen do if she were asked to sign her name? How could she hide her beardless face? What if their owners sent slave hunters after them? And if by some miracle they succeeded, she might never see her mother again! William offered just one argument: Didn't she want to raise a family in freedom? Those were the magic words. "I think it is almost too much for us to undertake," Ellen finally told her husband. "However, I will try to carry out the plan."

The couple immediately began to assemble Ellen's costume. She sewed a pair of men's trousers for herself. William took some of the money they had saved during their two years of marriage and visited various stores in Macon.

By selling goods to William, the shopkeepers were breaking the law, for slaves required their owners' permission to make purchases. But since slaves weren't allowed to testify in court, merchants generally did business with them without fear of getting in trouble. At one store, William bought a top hat for Ellen and a beaver hat for himself. Elsewhere he purchased her cloak, boots, and other clothing. Ellen then sent William to another shop to buy green spectacles to cover her eyes. To hide her beardless face, she wrapped a "toothache handkerchief" around her chin.

The greatest danger was that their owners would soon miss them and send slave hunters after them. The Crafts thought of a solution to this problem, too. At Christmastime, owners sometimes issued passes to their most trusted slaves so they could visit friends and relatives for a few days. Ellen had faithfully served Eliza Collins as a maid for 11 years. She asked her half-sister for permission to visit a sick relative who lived 12 miles from Macon. At first her mistress refused, but when Ellen burst into tears Mrs. Collins wrote out the pass she wanted. William persuaded Mr. Taylor to write a similar pass for him so he could accompany Ellen. Their passes were good for only three or four days. Be back in Macon by Christmas, their owners ordered Ellen and William.

But December 20 arrived—the eve of their departure—and one huge obstacle remained. If asked, Ellen wouldn't be able to sign her name, which would make people suspect that she was really a slave. The Crafts were beginning to think they might have to give up their plan when Ellen said, "I think I have it! I can bind up my right arm in a sling, and ask the officers to register my name for me!" By pretending to have arthritis, "Mr. Johnson" would then have an excuse to ask someone to sign for him.

That night they were too excited to sleep. They spent most of the dark hours planning how to deal with various dangers that might arise. Then, early Thursday morning, four days before Christmas, they left their cabin and began the journey that would result in their freedom—or their doom.

CENTRAL RAIL-ROAD.

FROM
SAVANNAH TO MACON, GEORGIA.

This ROAD is open from Savannah to "McCalls' Mill," 187½ miles from Savannah, and 2½ miles from the Depot at Macon, for transportation daily, (Sundays excepted.) The Mail and Passenger Train, will run to and from McCalls' Mill, on and after the first day of August next. The Road will be finished and opened to the Macon Depot in October next.

PASSAGE FOR 187½ MILES.

In Passenger Car, ... $8 00
" Baggage " 5 00

Children under 12 years, half price.

The Trains will leave (until further notice) as follows:—
Leave Savannah, at 6, A. M. and leave McCalls', at 6, A. M.

The Charleston Steamers will leave Savannah every Tuesday, Thursday and Saturday evenings, after the arrival of the trains.

August 1

CHAPTER THREE

THE FIRST
THOUSAND MILES

In their separate compartments, Ellen and William waited with pounding hearts for the train to depart. Any second, they feared, someone they knew would arrive at the Macon railway station, board the train, and recognize them. A minute or two before departure, it appeared that their worst nightmare was about to come true.

Peeking out the window of the Negro car, William saw the cabinetmaker for whom he worked talking to the ticket agent. Something had aroused his suspicions, so he had come to the station searching for William. As the cabinetmaker peered through the train windows, William slumped down in his seat with his hat covering his face as though he were sleeping. Just as the cabinetmaker approached the Negro car, the conductor rang his bell, and the train chugged out of the station.

Meanwhile, a man named Mr. Cray had boarded a whites-only car at the last moment. When he sat down right next to her, Ellen had the sinking feeling that Mr. Cray had been sent for the specific purpose of seizing her and bringing her home. He was a close friend of the Collinses. Not only had he known Ellen since her childhood, but she had served him dinner at the Collins home only the day before! It didn't seem possible to Ellen that she could fool Mr. Cray.

The train had gone a short way when Mr. Cray said to Ellen, "It is a fine morning, sir."

An 1843 announcement of the opening of a new route on the Georgia Central Railroad linking Macon to Savannah, Georgia. Ellen and William Craft began their journey on this train.

Ellen was convinced that, even if her costume had fooled Mr. Cray, he would recognize her voice. She did the only thing she could think of. Pretending to be deaf, she continued staring out the window.

"It is a *very* fine morning, sir!" Mr. Cray repeated in a louder voice. When Ellen still didn't respond, the other passengers laughed, embarrassing Mr. Cray.

"I will *make* him hear!" Mr. Cray said, and then yelled: *"It is a very fine morning, sir!"*

No longer able to ignore him, Ellen answered "Yes" in her lowest voice, then turned back toward the window.

Another man in the train car commented that the young gentleman suffering from toothache and arthritis must also be afflicted with deafness. "Yes," replied Mr. Cray, "and I shall not trouble him any more." As long as Mr. Cray sat next to her, Ellen's heart pounded so hard that she was afraid he would hear it. She finally caught her breath when Mr. Cray stepped off the train at a nearby town without showing any sign of having recognized her.

As the train puffed along at about 20 miles per hour, Ellen listened to the other passengers' conversations. She later told William that the white people

From the windows of the train, the Crafts might have seen other slaves living the life they were trying to leave behind. These slave houses were in Savannah, Georgia.

talked incessantly about three topics: "niggers, cotton, and the damned abolitionists." Ellen learned something from their talk. Abolitionists were not monsters; they were people who wanted to outlaw slavery.

Hour after hour, the train threaded its way past red clay hills and piney woods, cotton fields and slave cabins, small towns and swampland. Late that afternoon, when they approached the seacoast, Ellen and William saw slaves working in the rice fields. At 8 P.M., they arrived in Savannah, Georgia, after a train trip of more than 12 hours.

Having barely slept the previous night, the Crafts were extremely tired, but they couldn't stop to rest in Savannah. William hailed a carriage for himself and his "master," as he always referred to Ellen during their journey. The driver took them to the waterfront, where Ellen bought tickets for "William Johnson and slave" to travel by steamboat to Charleston, South Carolina.

William followed his wife up the gangplank of the *General Clinch*. Once they were aboard, a steward showed Mr. Johnson to a berth. The captain and some of the passengers were curious about the sickly young gentleman who had disappeared into his cabin. They surrounded William and barraged him with questions about his master. He had better prove that Mr. Johnson wasn't well, William realized, so he took out a medicated bandage they had brought along in their suitcase and heated it at the stove in the vessel's dining room.

The medicated bandage smelled so awful that a man in the dining room demanded, "Buck, what have you got there?"

"Opodeldoc, sir," answered William. That was what people of the time called a medicated dressing for arthritis.

"I should think it's opo-*devil*," remarked a thin young man, who was leaning back in a chair. "It stinks enough to kill or cure 20 men!" he added, spitting out a wad of tobacco. "Away with it, or I will throw it overboard!"

William took the opodeldoc bandage to Ellen's cabin, which seemed to convince the passengers that shy young Mr. Johnson was suffering from a serious case of arthritis. William then went and asked the steward where he could sleep.

"There is no place on this vessel for colored passengers to sleep, whether they are slave or free," the steward answered. Most of that night, William paced the deck beneath the stars. Before dawn, when everyone else was

*A steamboat at a landing in Georgia in the mid-1800s;
the Crafts boarded a vessel like this in Savannah.*

asleep, he climbed onto some cotton bags near the steamboat's funnel and managed to get a couple hours of sleep.

Still curious about Mr. Johnson, the captain invited the handsomely dressed young man to eat breakfast at his table. Ordinarily, William wouldn't have been allowed at the table with white people, but Mr. Johnson explained that he couldn't use his right arm and required his slave's assistance to eat. As William stood by and cut up the food, Mr. Johnson let him take a few scraps for himself.

The captain watched William help his master eat, then advised Mr. Johnson: "You have a very attentive boy, sir. But you had better watch him like a hawk when you get on to the North. He seems all very well here, but he may act quite differently there. I know several gentlemen who have lost their valuable niggers among them damned cutthroat abolitionists."

A slave dealer eating a large piece of chicken for breakfast added his advice. "I would not take a nigger to the North under no consideration. I have had a lot to do with niggers in my time, but I never saw one who had his heel on free soil that was worth a damn. Now, stranger," he said to Mr. Johnson, "If you have made up your mind to sell this here nigger, I am your man. Just mention your price, and I will pay for him with hard silver dollars. What do you say, stranger?" He stared at Mr. Johnson with bloodshot eyes and awaited his response.

Slave dealers like this man had been selling William and Ellen's people for generations. William, who was a big, powerful man, felt like throwing the slave dealer overboard. And Ellen, who had heard her half-sister tell people off, wanted to call him an ignorant boor each time he used the word "nigger." But the Crafts had foreseen situations such as this and knew they couldn't draw attention to themselves by losing their tempers. William looked away so the man wouldn't see the anger in his eyes. Ellen politely said, "I don't wish to sell him sir. I cannot get on well without him."

"You will *have* to get on without him if you take him to the North," insisted the slave dealer. "I can see from the look in his eyes that he is certain to run away."

"I think not, sir," answered Mr. Johnson. "I have great confidence in his fidelity."

Frustrated at being unable to convince Mr. Johnson to sell William, the slave dealer slammed his fist so hard on the table that he spilled a cup of hot coffee into another man's lap. "It always makes me mad to hear a man talking about fidelity in niggers," he said. "There isn't a damned one of them who wouldn't run away if he had half a chance."

A young southern Army officer also had some advice for Mr. Johnson. Having observed how politely the young gentleman spoke to his slave, the Army officer warned, "Nothing spoils a slave so soon as saying 'thank you' and 'if you please' to him. The only way to make a nigger toe the mark and keep him in his place is to storm at him like thunder."

To demonstrate, the officer called his slave to him and swore ferociously at him for no reason. "*That* is the way to speak to them," said the officer. "If every nigger was drilled in this manner, they would be as humble as dogs, and never dare to run away."

The *General Clinch* soon docked at Charleston, ending the conversation, but the runaways didn't leave the vessel with the other passengers. By this time, they feared, their owners might have learned of their escape and telegraphed to Charleston offering a reward for their capture. Someone in the crowd on the dock might be a slave catcher on the lookout for them. Ellen and William waited until everyone else had left the *General Clinch* and the dock had emptied before slipping off quietly.

Before resuming their journey, the Crafts stopped at a Charleston hotel for something to eat. Mr. Johnson was directed into the elegant dining room, while William was fed leftovers in the kitchen. It may have been during their stop at the hotel that the couple heard distressing news. Having eavesdropped on white people's conversations back in Macon, they had believed that from Charleston they could take a single steamboat to Philadelphia and freedom. Now they discovered that the vessel didn't operate in the wintertime. Instead they would have to take a series of steamboats and trains to the North.

The couple left the hotel and returned to the waterfront. They entered the steamboat office and approached the counter where a mean-looking port official with cheese-colored skin was sitting. Ellen took out her money to purchase two tickets for "William Johnson and slave" to travel to Philadelphia by steamboat and train.

The Crafts didn't know it, but as one of the nation's leading slave markets, Charleston had strict rules about taking black people out of the city. The official carefully studied Mr. Johnson and his slave. "Boy, do you belong to this gentleman?" he demanded of William.

"Yes, sir," William replied.

"Where did you come from?"

"Atlanta, Georgia, sir," said William, hoping to put the official on the wrong trail if he decided to send a telegraph message inquiring about runaway slaves.

After Ellen paid for the tickets, the official shoved a ledger book onto the counter and said, "I wish you to register your name here, sir, and also the name of your nigger, and pay a dollar duty on him."

Mr. Johnson quickly produced the dollar, but, pointing to his crippled arm, he asked the official to sign for him.

Perhaps Mr. Johnson's voice or light brown skin made the port official suspicious, for he snapped back, "I shan't do it!" Mr. Johnson would have to find a way to sign for himself.

By this time, the passengers in line behind the Crafts were watching intently to see what would happen next. Several of them prodded Mr.

Johnson to sign his name as best he could, using his left hand if need be. Realizing that they were trapped, Ellen and William were staring at one another in despair when unexpected help appeared.

The young Army officer who had earlier advised Mr. Johnson to be cruel to his slave entered the steamboat office and saw what was happening. He had been drinking, and when he staggered up to them Ellen and William could smell liquor on his breath. With the gallantry of one Southern gentleman to another, he declared that Mr. Johnson was his friend. "I know his family like a book!" he asserted.

The Army officer was well known in Charleston, so the steamboat captain, who had overheard the dispute, also stepped forward gallantly. "I'll register the gentleman's name and take the responsibility," he offered, writing *Mr. Johnson and Slave* in the ledger book. The port official reluctantly handed Mr. Johnson the precious tickets that would allow him to travel with his slave all the way to Philadelphia.

The Crafts' journey continued with a steamboat trip up the Carolina coast. Once the steamer was heading northward, its captain, who had signed for Mr. Johnson in Charleston, apologized to the young gentleman for his trouble in the office that morning. "It was not out of any disrespect to you, sir," he explained.

The harbor at Charleston, South Carolina, as the Crafts would have seen it when they boarded a steamer bound for Wilmington, North Carolina.

"They make it a rule to be very strict at Charleston. If they were not very careful, any damned abolitionist might take off a lot of valuable niggers."

"I suppose so," Mr. Johnson said, and then thanked the captain for his help.

The next morning—Saturday, December 23, the third day of their journey—the steamer arrived at Wilmington, North Carolina. There, the Crafts boarded a train bound for Richmond, Virginia.

<hr/>

"They make it a rule to be very strict at Charleston. If they were not very careful, any damned abolitionist might take off a lot of valuable niggers."

<hr/>

Riding in separate train cars once again, Ellen and William felt their hopes rise and fall like the hilly land beneath them. When their train crossed from North Carolina into Virginia late on the 23rd, they were roughly two-thirds of the way through their thousand-mile journey. Yet the longer they were gone, the greater was the chance that their plot had been uncovered. There were many ways this could have happened.

Might a storekeeper have revealed William's unusual purchases? Had someone observed them walking to the Macon railway station? Did the cabinetmaker discover that William had been on the Georgia Central? What if Ellen's costume hadn't fooled Mr. Cray after all?

Once convinced that Ellen and William *had* run away, their owners could have telegraphed messages throughout the South offering rewards for their capture. Plenty of slave hunters would be eager for the reward money, which could total hundreds of dollars, the equivalent of thousands of dollars today. So as the train moved on through Virginia, Ellen and William kept an eye on each new passenger who boarded. If they spotted anyone who seemed to be searching for them, they would have to get off the train and continue on foot.

One problem was: how would they recognize a slave hunter? Another was that with each passing hour, the couple found it more difficult to remain alert. They had now gone three days with little food or sleep, and it took all of their will power to keep their eyes open, especially with the clickety-clack, clickety-clack of the train wheels and the rhythmic rocking of the passenger cars.

When the train stopped at Petersburg, 40 miles south of Richmond, Virginia, a planter and his two beautiful daughters took seats near Ellen. The three newcomers felt an immediate sympathy for the sickly young gentleman, and asked where he was from and where he was headed.

"What seems to be the matter with you, sir, may I be allowed to ask?" inquired the father. Upon learning that the malady was arthritis, he took out a pen and paper and wrote out what he called a "cure" for the disease. Ellen thanked him and immediately placed the paper in her pocket, for if she happened to look at it upside-down, they would realize she couldn't read. The daughters fussed over Mr. Johnson and made a pillow out of their shawls so he could take a nap. To avoid further conversation, Ellen lay down on the seat and closed her eyes.

As the girls hovered over Ellen, one of them sighed and said, "Papa, he seems to be a very nice young gentleman!" The other daughter added, "Oh, dear me, I never felt so much for a gentleman in all my life!"

Ellen pretended to sleep, all the while dreading that the girls would suddenly realize their mistake. In her mind she could hear their screams of horror when they realized they had been flirting with a runaway slave woman rather than a white man. But the train rolled on, and still the young ladies and their father didn't suspect Ellen's true identity. Finally, they arrived at Richmond, where Ellen and William were to change trains. The young ladies were sad to part with their new friend at the Richmond railway station, but Ellen could barely hide her relief.

The Crafts met on the platform, then hurried to the train that would take them on the next leg of their journey. Ellen boarded first and was soon joined by a plump elderly woman who sat nearby. As she gazed out the window, the elderly lady saw something that made her spring to her feet. "Bless my soul," she said. "There goes my nigger, Ned!"

Ellen glanced out the window and saw that the woman was talking about William, who was passing along the platform on his way to the Negro car. "No, that is *my* boy!" Ellen protested.

But the woman poked her head out the window and ordered, "You, Ned, come to me, sir, you runaway rascal!" Only when William turned to face her did she realize her mistake. "I beg your pardon, sir," she told Mr. Johnson. "I was sure it was my nigger. I was as kind to him as if he had been my own son but he ran off without any cause whatever."

Ellen disliked this woman so intensely that she forgot she and William had agreed to avoid talking to their fellow passengers if possible. "When did Ned leave you?" she asked.

It turned out that the woman had sold Ned's wife to a New Orleans slave dealer after she couldn't work in the fields any longer due to illness. Ned had run off to try to find her. "The ungrateful wretches are always running away," said the woman, who revealed that, on his deathbed, her husband had realized slavery was wicked and had willed all his slaves free. "But I knew he was too good a man to do such an unkind thing, had he been in his right mind," said the woman, "and therefore I had the will altered."

Before she knew it, the words spilled out of Ellen's mouth. "Do you mean, madam," Mr. Johnson angrily demanded, "that willing the slaves free was unkind to them, or costly to yourself?"

"To the slaves!" replied the woman with annoyance. "It seems cruel to turn niggers loose to shift for themselves, when there are so many good masters to take care of them."

That remark prompted a young Southern gentleman seated near Ellen to criticize the woman for not freeing her slaves as her husband had wanted. Ellen had an opinion, but she had said too much already, so she held her tongue. When the woman left the train, the Southern gentleman said what Ellen was thinking: "What a damned shame for that old whining humbug to cheat the poor Negroes out of their liberty!" This was the first time Ellen had heard a white Southerner sympathize with slaves.

Near Fredericksburg, Virginia, the fugitive couple left the train and took a steamboat up the Potomac River toward Washington, D.C. On the vessel with Ellen and William were a number of slave owners from the Washington area, for the national capital was a Southern city and would allow slavery until 1862.

As they steamed up the Potomac, a planter kept staring at William and his master with disgust. Finally, he tried to pick a fight with Mr. Johnson.

Their owners promised a reward for the capture and return of this runaway slave family.

"You are spoiling your nigger by letting him wear such a devilish fine hat," he said. "The President couldn't wear a better hat! I should like to kick it over-board. I'd like to get hold of every damned nigger I see dressed like a white man and sell every damned rascal way down South, where the devil would be whipped out of them."

Ellen had learned her lesson with the old woman. Refusing to be drawn into an argument, she turned and walked away, leaving the planter cursing to himself.

A few minutes later the steamer landed at Washington, D.C. It was now the afternoon of Sunday, December 24—Christmas Eve—and the nation's capital was decked out in its holiday finery. Ellen and William stopped only briefly in the city, for Washington always had a number of slave catchers prowling about. The Crafts hailed the first carriage they could find and headed straight to the railway station, where they boarded the train for Baltimore, Maryland.

It took the train about two hours to cover the 40 miles between Washington and Baltimore. Ellen and William were exhausted from nearly four days of travel, but as they walked toward the northbound train at the Baltimore station they trembled with excitement. All that remained now was a 50-mile train ride to the most glorious spot on Earth: the free soil of Pennsylvania.

*Slaves in chains being herded through Washington, D.C., in the early 1800s.
The U.S. capital permitted slavery until 1862.*

William helped Mr. Johnson onto a train car and was stepping into the Negro car when a station official tapped him on the shoulder and demanded, "Where are you going, boy?"

"To Philadelphia, sir," William answered.

"What are you going there for?"

"I am traveling with my master, who is in the next carriage, sir."

"Well," said the official, "I calculate you had better get him out, and be mighty quick about it, because the train will soon be starting. It is against the rules to let any man take a slave past here unless he can satisfy them in the office that he has a right to take him along."

William knew what the words "satisfy them in the office" meant. Mr.

Johnson would be asked to produce papers proving that William was his property, just as people today have papers showing that they own a house or a car. Of course, Ellen had no such papers. William felt his heart thumping wildly as he entered his wife's compartment to tell her the bad news.

He found her seated at one end of the car apart from the other passengers. She looked up, saw William, and smiled, confident that they were a few hours from freedom. William tried to act cheerful, so as not to attract attention. "How do you feel, sir," he asked, loud enough for the other passengers to hear.

"Much better," Mr. Johnson answered. Then she whispered to her husband, "Thank God we are getting on so nicely."

"I'm afraid, sir," William whispered, "we are not getting on quite so well as we had anticipated."

"What is the matter?" asked Ellen, starting to panic. When he explained the situation, Ellen looked crushed. "Good heavens, William!" she whispered. "Is it possible that we are doomed to hopeless bondage after all?"

Their hearts were too heavy for them to say anything more for a minute or two. There was no running now, they knew. They could not get far on foot, for Baltimore was closely patrolled for runaway slaves. Their only hope was for Mr. Johnson to talk his way out of this predicament. They told one another to be brave, then stepped off the train together. Doing their best to appear calm, they walked to the station office.

"Do you wish to see me, sir?" Mr. Johnson asked the man in charge.

"Yes," he answered. "It is against our rules, sir, to allow any person to take a slave out of Baltimore into Philadelphia unless he can satisfy us that he has a right to take him along."

"Why is that?" asked Mr. Johnson, with a firmness that surprised even her husband.

"Because, sir," continued the official, "if we allow any gentleman to take a slave past here into Philadelphia, and should the gentleman turn out not to be his rightful owner, and should the proper master come and prove that his slave escaped on our road, we shall have to pay him. Therefore, we cannot let any slave pass here without proof that it is all right."

Did Mr. Johnson have papers proving that he owned this slave?

No, answered Mr. Johnson, he had left the papers at home.

Did he know anyone in Baltimore who could vouch for the fact that William was his slave? No, repeated Mr. Johnson, he was a stranger in the city.

"Well, sir," said the official, "I can't let you go."

Ellen knew that what she said next could determine whether she and her husband would live out their lives as free people or as slaves. Staring icily at the official through the green glasses, Mr. Johnson said, in a commanding tone, "I bought tickets in Charleston to pass us through to Philadelphia, and therefore you have no right to detain us here."

The other passengers in the office began clamoring for the official to allow the sickly gentleman to continue his journey. As the bell rang signaling that the train was about to depart, everyone looked at the official to see what he would decide. "I really don't know what to do," he said, and then suddenly made up his mind. "As he is not well, it is a pity to stop him here. We will let him go."

The Crafts hurried onto the platform, where Ellen entered a first-class compartment and William was sent to the baggage car just before the train rolled out of the station. They were so fatigued from four days and three nights on the run that William fell into a deep sleep before the train reached Havre de Grace, Maryland, a town on the broad Susquehanna River.

The train rolled to a stop near the river, and the passengers were told that they must get off. They and their luggage were to be ferried across the Susquehanna to a train waiting on the opposite shore. It was dark and raining at that late hour. As she crossed the river in the ferryboat with the other passengers, Ellen looked for William. Her husband was nowhere to be seen. A mere 20 miles from the free soil of Pennsylvania, William seemed to have vanished.

‌

As she crossed the river in the ferryboat
with the other passengers,
Ellen looked for William.
Her husband was nowhere to be seen.

After the passengers and their luggage were transported across the river, Mr. Johnson asked the conductor if he had seen his slave. "No, sir," the conductor answered. "I have no doubt he has run away, and is in Philadelphia, free, long before now."

Ellen knew that William hadn't run off. Something terrible must have happened. Someone had murdered her husband and he was lying at the bottom of the Susquehanna. Or a slave hunter had captured him and was taking him back to Macon. But just before the train began moving, a guard found William asleep in the luggage car.

"Boy, wake up, your master is scared half to death about you!" said the guard, shaking him violently. No one had bothered to awaken William when the baggage had been ferried across the Susquehanna. He had been so exhausted that he had slept through being moved with the trunks.

William rushed into Ellen's car to show her that he hadn't disappeared. Upon seeing her husband, Ellen could barely hold back her tears of joy.

Once William was back in the baggage car, the guard returned to talk to him. "Let me give you a little friendly advice," said the guard. "When you get to Philadelphia, run away and leave that cripple, and have your liberty."

The guard seemed astonished when William answered, "I shall never run away from such a good master as I have at present." William also met a black man on the train whom he couldn't fool. He knew William was an escaped slave, the man said. He recommended that William go to a Philadelphia rooming house that was run by an abolitionist.

William and Ellen couldn't help falling asleep as the train continued northward. Sometime during the night they crossed the border onto the free soil of Pennsylvania. Toward dawn, the train blew its whistle so loudly that William and Ellen both awoke with a start in their separate cars. Through their windows they could see the flickering lights of Philadelphia.

Even before the train wheels stopped turning, William rushed into his wife's compartment. Ellen was so weak from the strain and hardships of their journey that her husband had to help her walk to a carriage.

"Thank God, William, we are safe," said Ellen, as they rode toward the abolitionist's rooming house. The sun rose that Christmas morning on a young couple who were, for the first time in their lives, free.

THIRD STREET, PHILADELPHIA,—SHOWING THE LEDGER, AND JAYNE'S BUILDINGS.

CHAPTER FOUR

THE CITY
OF
BROTHERLY LOVE

The landlord showed the Crafts to their room. Once alone, the couple knelt down, much as they had four mornings earlier on the floor of their slave cabin a thousand miles to the south. "Thank you, Lord," they said, "for your goodness in enabling us to escape out of the jaws of the wicked." Ellen then opened their suitcase and changed into her dress. When they came downstairs into the sitting room, the landlord stared at Ellen in disbelief.

"Where is your master?" the landlord demanded of William, who pointed to his wife. Growing annoyed, the landlord repeated: "I am not joking! I wish to see your master!" Again, William pointed to Ellen.

"That is not the gentleman who came in with you!" said the landlord.

The couple explained that they had just escaped from slavery with Ellen disguised as a white man. But not until she showed him her costume did he fully believe their story.

A religious group called the Quakers had founded Philadelphia and given the city its name, which means *Brotherly Love*. True believers that all people are created equal, the Quakers had long been among the country's leading opponents of slavery. Philadelphia also had a large population of "free blacks," as the twelve percent of all African Americans who were not slaves were called.

Over the next few days, their landlord introduced the Crafts to Quakers, free blacks, and other abolitionists who were eager to hear about their

Philadelphia, Pennsylvania, as it appeared around the time the Crafts arrived. The city was the gateway to freedom for thousands of runaway slaves.

escape and see Ellen in her costume. Among the people the Crafts met was William Still, a free black man from New Jersey who, as a leader of the Pennsylvania Anti-Slavery Society, helped hundreds of escaped slaves. But no fugitive made a deeper impression on Still than the Crafts. Years later, in his book *The Underground Railroad,* Still recalled meeting the couple:

> *Never can [I] forget the impression made by their arrival. [They were] in a private room surrounded by a few friends—Ellen in her fine suit of black, with her cloak and high-heeled boots, looking, in every respect, like a young gentleman. In an hour, after having dropped her male attire, and assumed the [clothing] of her sex, the feminine only was visible in [her] every line and feature.*

The Crafts also met William Wells Brown in the City of Brotherly Love. Formerly a slave in Missouri, Brown had escaped during the winter of 1833–1834 and become an Underground Railroad conductor—a person who led fugitive slaves to freedom. While working on steamboats, Brown had helped transport many runaway slaves to Canada—as many as 69 in a single year. Brown was also an author. His *Narrative of William Wells Brown, A Fugitive Slave* had appeared in 1847. A few years later he would write *Clotel; or, The President's Daughter,* the first novel by an African American. Brown and the Crafts quickly became friends. Shortly after the couple's arrival on free soil, Brown wrote a letter about them that appeared on January 12, 1849, in *The Liberator,* an anti-slavery newspaper William Lloyd Garrison published in Boston, Massachusetts.

As the news of their escape spread, the Crafts became famous. People especially marveled at Ellen, who had been so brave, risking discovery at every moment. News of the couple's escape reached the South, too, and enraged white slave owners. A few days earlier, the Crafts had been mere property, without a right in the world. Now Northern abolitionists were portraying them as heroes who had outwitted their evil masters.

Although runaways were free once they stepped on free soil, they could still lose their liberty. In 1793, the United States had passed a fugitive slave law enabling owners to capture and take back their runaways. Usually owners did not try to seize fugitive slaves once they reached the North, for it was-

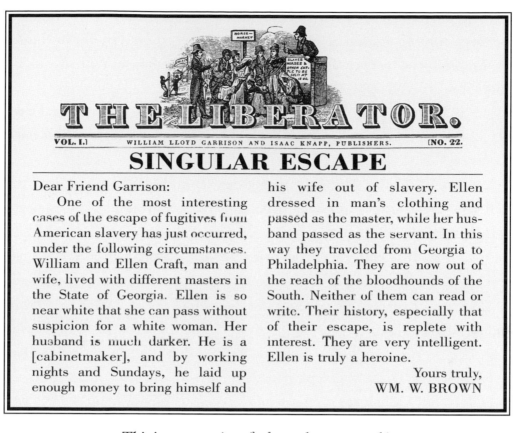

*This is a re-creation of a letter that appeared in
The Liberator on January 12, 1849*

n't worth the expense to send slave hunters that far. But as symbols of the anti-slavery movement, the Crafts were a special case. Southerners were eager to chase down the famous fugitives to show that the South had the right to continue slavery.

Their new abolitionist friends realized that slave hunters could easily find the famous couple in Philadelphia and force them back into bondage. Barclay Ivens, a Quaker whom the Crafts had met briefly, invited them to stay at his home 25 miles outside Philadelphia. Around New Year's Day of 1849, Ellen and William traveled by steamboat up the Delaware River to the Ivens farm.

When the Crafts arrived at the farm and Ellen saw the family waiting by the doorway, she grew very nervous. Because Mr. Ivens was rather dark, Ellen had assumed that he and his family were African Americans. Now she realized her mistake. Mr. and Mrs. Ivens and their three daughters and son were white.

William walked toward the house, but Ellen pulled him back. "I thought we were coming among colored people," she whispered to her husband.

Embarrassed by his wife's reluctance to enter the house, William quietly answered, "It is all right, they are the same."

"No!" Ellen insisted, "It is *not* all right, and I am *not* going to stop here. I have no confidence whatever in white people. They are only trying to get us back to slavery!"

Sensing Ellen's fear, Mrs. Ivens rushed out. "Don't be frightened, Ellen," she said in motherly tones, "I shall not hurt a single hair of thy head. We have heard with much pleasure of the marvelous escape of thee and thy husband, and deeply sympathize with thee in all that thou hast undergone. Thou need not fear us. We would as soon send one of our own daughters into slavery as thee."

In Ellen's 22 years of life, never before had a white person spoken to her with such tenderness. Suddenly she burst into tears. Ellen later told William that she had cried because for the first time she realized that "there are good and bad persons of every shade of complexion."

Ellen and William ate supper with the Ivens family. When the meal was finished, the Ivenses asked the Crafts whether they could read or write. Somewhere they had learned how to say the alphabet, they answered, but they did not know how to write the letters, let alone read or write any words. Moreover, they were convinced that they were too old to learn. Nonsense, their hosts insisted. As soon as the dishes were cleared away, they took out spelling books and writing slates and began teaching the Crafts the alphabet.

During the next two weeks or so, this kind Quaker family fed, sheltered, and tutored the fugitive couple. Ellen and William proved to be fast learners and were soon able to write their names and read simple words.

But then their abolitionist friends from Philadelphia warned the Crafts that it was time for them to move on. Pennsylvania was too near the slave states for such famous fugitives to make it their permanent home.

Boston was the place for the Crafts to settle, their friends advised. Bostonians had a long history of fighting for what they believed. Back in the 1770s, Bostonians had helped ignite the struggle for American independence. The Boston Massacre, the Boston Tea Party, and the battles at Lexington and Concord that had started the Revolution had all taken place in or near the city.

Now, about 75 years later, Bostonians were spearheading the fight against slavery. In fact, by 1849 many Americans feared that Bostonians' anti-slavery stance would set off a civil war between North and South.

Several Bostonians were among the nation's most prominent abolitionists. William Lloyd Garrison, publisher of *The Liberator,* was despised so intensely by Southerners that the state of Georgia offered a $5,000 reward to anyone who could arrest and convict him of a crime in connection with his anti-slavery work. That would equal about $100,000 in today's money. Other Bostonians noted for their opposition to slavery included Theodore Parker, a minister who was eager for a war to free the slaves, and social reformer Wendell Phillips, who wanted the North to separate from the South. Thousands of Boston's working people were eager to fight any slave hunters who came to their city. If there was any place in the United States where the Crafts would be safe, it was Boston.

William Wells Brown proposed a plan. People were eager to meet Ellen and William and hear their story. Brown offered to accompany the Crafts to Boston and then take them on a lecture tour of Massachusetts and nearby states. Besides stirring up anti-slavery sentiment, the tour would raise money for the abolitionist movement and for the Crafts. The couple would then have some funds when they were ready to settle down to a normal life in Boston. Ellen and William liked their new friend's idea.

In January of 1849, the Crafts said good-bye to Mr. and Mrs. Ivens and their children. About two weeks earlier, Ellen had arrived at the Ivens farm with a heart filled with suspicion. Both she and her husband departed feeling that they were leaving their dearest friends in the world.

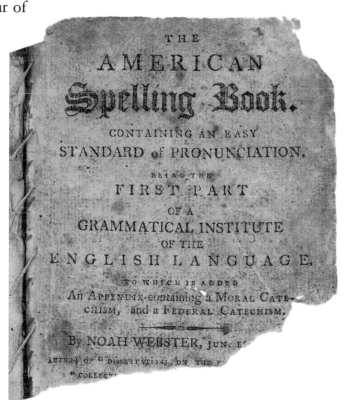

THE AMERICAN Spelling Book.

CONTAINING AN EASY STANDARD of PRONUNCIATION.

BEING THE FIRST PART OF A GRAMMATICAL INSTITUTE OF THE ENGLISH LANGUAGE.

TO WHICH IS ADDED An APPENDIX containing a MORAL CATECHISM, and a FEDERAL CATECHISM.

BY NOAH WEBSTER, JUN. E

The Crafts probably used this speller for their lessons with the Ivens family.

CHAPTER FIVE

THE CRADLE
OF
LIBERTY

Having discovered that escaping a thousand miles from Georgia wasn't far enough, the Crafts traveled with William Wells Brown another 300 miles north to Boston. They were hailed as heroes the moment they stepped off the train in the Massachusetts capital.

Soon after their arrival, Ellen and William attended a Massachusetts Anti-Slavery Society rally at Boston's Faneuil Hall. The building was known as the "Cradle of Liberty" because of the gatherings to promote American independence that had once been held there. A huge crowd cheered as the Crafts entered the hall. At this meeting, Wendell Phillips called their escape "an incident of courage and noble daring." Phillips predicted that "future historians and poets will tell their story as one of the most thrilling tales in the nation's annals, and millions will read it with admiration."

After a short stay in Boston, which was where Brown now lived, he and the Crafts began their tour. Traveling by train and stagecoach, over the next four months they spoke in more than 60 New England towns, including Worcester, Brookfield, Springfield, Lowell, Salem, and New Bedford, Massachusetts; Pawtucket, Rhode Island; and Norwich, Connecticut.

The first aerial photograph ever taken in the United States, this balloon view of Boston dates from 1860.

Crowds gathered to hear the three former slaves in town halls and other meeting places. William Wells Brown would make an abolitionist speech, sing a few anti-slavery songs, and introduce "the Georgia Fugitives." William would relate the story of their escape while Ellen modeled her now-famous disguise. The program ended with the collection of funds to benefit the Crafts and the anti-slavery campaign.

Women of that era rarely spoke in public, but in Northborough, Massachusetts, the audience demanded, "Let us hear Mrs. Craft!" Ellen only answered a few questions at first, but gradually, she joined in retelling the story of their escape.

Many people in the Crafts' position would have relished the money and fame that came with their lecture tour. But Ellen and William wanted only to settle into regular jobs, buy a home, and start a family. They repeatedly announced that they were giving up the tour, but each time William Wells Brown and other abolitionists insisted that they must "go on for the good of the cause."

Finally, in May of 1849 the Crafts followed their own desires and returned to Boston—permanently, they hoped. They moved into a boarding-house at 66 Phillips Street that was operated by Harriet and Lewis Hayden, another fugitive slave couple who became their close friends.

Next the Crafts found work. William opened his own little shop on Federal Street where he made cabinets and sold used furniture. Ellen had no trouble finding employment as a seamstress. Some of Boston's wealthiest families hired her to make clothing for them in their mansions on Beacon Hill.

Meanwhile, newspapers had been carrying stories about Ellen and William. In early 1849, the *New Haven Register* featured a story about the couple's appearance before the Massachusetts Anti-Slavery Society in Boston, and the *Boston Post* ran an article in which William Wells Brown described their escape. Newspapers of that time routinely copied stories from other papers. On February 13, 1849, the *Georgia Telegraph* in Macon published a story headlined "Runaway Slaves." It repeated the *New Haven Register* and *Boston Post* articles. The *Georgia Telegraph* then added a paragraph of its own, mistakenly adding an "s" to the couple's name.

The Georgia Telegraph

MACON, GA., TUESDAY MORNING, FEBRUARY 13, 1849

RUNAWAY SLAVES

The following is from the *New Haven Register* of the 3d inst:

A good-looking mulatto man, and a still better looking almost white girl, with straight hair, lately escaped from their master in Georgia, and reached Boston as man and wife. At the annual meeting of the Massachusetts Anti-Slavery Society, held in Boston, last week, this couple were seated upon the platform—and a Mr. Brown, (who had also taken French leave of Kentucky, and who remarked that he did not feel above common white folks, although his father was one of the aristocracy of that State), gave the audience some anecdotes relative to the escape of the happy couple—she being dressed as a gentleman planter, attended by her servant. The *Boston Post* thus reports Mr. Brown:

"Fashionably dressed as a buck of the highest ton, with her arm in a sling, Mrs. Crafts was the object of much tender sympathy in the cars, particularly on the part of an elderly lady who was travelling with a marriageable daughter, who with a well managed sigh, remarked upon the languid appearance and distinguished air of the supposed young planter. Crafts, when asked the nature of his young master's indisposition, replied that he had been suffering from rheumatism, and a complication of diseases. An elderly gentleman thought the young gentleman would ride more comfortably, if his boots were taken off, and his feet extended across the seats; and before the interesting patient had time to express an opinion upon the subject, the kind-hearted old _____ had one of Mrs. Crafts boot in his hands! Perhaps he will recollect the incident, when he reads this account of it."

The Mr. and Mrs. Crafts who figure so largely in the above paragraph, will be recognized at once by our city readers as the slaves belonging to Dr. Collins and Mr. Ira H. Taylor, of this place, who runaway or were decoyed from their owners in December last.

A re-creation of an article about the Crafts' escape published in the Georgia Telegraph on February 13, 1849.

In one way, the Crafts were grateful to learn about this article in their hometown newspaper. Through word of mouth, Ellen's mother and their other relatives and friends would know that they were safe. But it also meant that their former owners now knew where to find them. In addition, by naming Dr. Collins and Mr. Taylor, the newspaper was challenging them to recapture their runaway slaves. It was a challenge they would not ignore.

A few months later, William was in his shop on Federal Street when the door opened. He looked up from his work and was startled to see Isaac

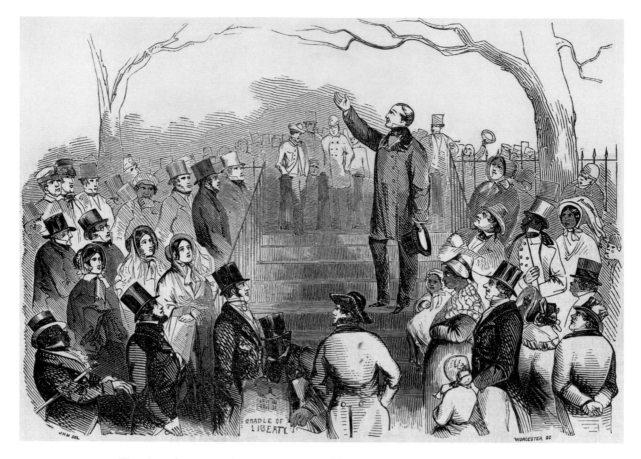

During the 1800s, Bostonians would gather in public places to hear abolitionists speak about the evils of slavery.

Scott, a white man from Georgia who owned one of William's brothers. Mr. Scott had a proposition: If William would pay him a large sum of money, he would free his brother.

Suspecting that Scott's offer was a fake, William turned it down. Scott's true mission, William soon learned, was to capture him and Ellen and return them to their former owners in Macon. William quickly closed his store. For a number of days thereafter, he and Ellen hid at a secret location in Boston. Once Scott realized that the Boston abolitionists would stop him if he tried to seize the Crafts, he gave up and returned home. William then opened a new store on Cambridge Street.

As the months passed and no more slave hunters appeared, William and Ellen felt more secure. Now and then "the Georgia Fugitives" attended abolitionist meetings where they were treated as celebrities. Each week they put away a little money. By 1850, when they had been in Boston for nearly two years, the Crafts had saved almost enough money to buy their own home. Ellen and William were grateful for each day of freedom and felt that a grand future awaited them.

Then, with a stroke of a pen, everything changed. Despite the abolitionist sentiment in places like Boston and Philadelphia, most Northerners were willing to compromise on slavery in order to avoid a civil war. Southerners generally felt the same way. In 1850 the United States Congress passed a series of acts intended to keep the peace between the North and the South. Known as the Compromise of 1850, the acts included admitting California as a Free State, which pleased the North. On September 18, 1850, President Millard Fillmore gave the South something in return by signing a new fugitive slave bill that made it easier for owners to recapture escaped slaves.

According to the new Fugitive Slave Law of 1850, federal marshals and other officials were required to assist white persons attempting to capture their runaway slaves. A key part of the law was Section 7, which specified that anyone who hid or assisted a runaway slave could be jailed for six months and fined $2,000:

> *Any persons who shall knowingly and willingly obstruct...[the capture of a fugitive slave]...or shall harbor or conceal such fugitive ...shall...be subject to a fine not exceeding one thousand dollars, and imprisonment not exceeding six months...and shall moreover forfeit and pay, by way of civil damages to the party injured by such illegal conduct, the sum of one thousand dollars, for each fugitive so lost...*

In 1833 the British Parliament had passed an act ending slavery throughout the British Empire as of the following year. This meant that slavery became illegal in Canada, which Britain then ruled. Within weeks of the signing of the new Fugitive Slave Law, hundreds of runaway slaves who had been living peacefully in Northern cities in the United States packed up and moved farther north into Canada. Despite Boston's reputation for protecting its black citizens, dozens fled that city, too. But dozens of others, including the Crafts, decided to remain in Boston and fight the new law.

Bostonians formed "vigilance committees" to protect escaped slaves. On October 4, 1850, just 16 days after President Fillmore signed the Fugitive Slave Law, black Bostonians gathered at the African Meeting House, a short way from the state capitol building. They organized the League of Freedom to resist the new law and "rescue and protect [fugitive] slaves at every hazard." Lewis Hayden was elected president and William Craft vice president of the organization.

A few days later, another protest meeting was held at Faneuil Hall. Its chairman, Charles Francis Adams, was the grandson of President John Adams and the son of President John Quincy Adams. Frederick Douglass, an escaped slave who had become a renowned author and civil rights leader, spoke at this meeting. Pointing at the Crafts, who were sitting on the platform, Douglass asked, "Will we permit a fugitive slave to be captured in Boston?"

"No!" came the crowd's thunderous response.

A Committee of Safety and Vigilance, headed by the Reverend Theodore Parker, was created at this meeting to protect black Bostonians from slave catchers. No one opposed the Fugitive Slave Law more than Reverend Parker, who claimed that it violated the "laws of God" and declared, "What is a fine of a thousand dollars, and jailing for six months, [compared] to the liberty of a man?" Little did they know then that Ellen and William would be the first of Boston's fugitives to be pursued under the new law.

Faneuil Hall in Boston, where Frederick Douglass challenged Bostonians to ignore the Fugitive Slave Law and protect escaped slaves.

The Crafts tried to maintain their usual routine during this troubling time.

They went to work, kept saving for a home, and planned to enroll in night school. However, ten days before Halloween of 1850, the long arm of the Fugitive Slave Law reached them in Boston.

William was in his furniture store on Cambridge Street when the bell rattled and a man walked in. William's heart sank. Approaching him was John Knight, a white man who had been employed with him in the cabinet shop back in Macon. Acting as though William was a long-lost friend, Knight said that he had come North to buy some machinery and had decided to drop in on the Crafts to say hello. He asked William to interrupt his work and show him around Boston, but William suspected that Knight had come to take him and Ellen back to Georgia.

"I have work to do and cannot go just now," explained William, pretending to be friendly. Then he casually asked, "Are you in Boston alone?"

"Yes. Nobody came with me," answered Knight. He spoke for a few minutes about people back in Macon before departing.

That night William told Ellen the bad news and asked her to stay inside their apartment until he learned more about Knight's intentions. William also bought a pistol, which he kept loaded and with him at all times.

The next day John Knight returned to William's shop. He repeated his request to be shown around the city, but once again William insisted he was too busy.

"Well, then," said Knight, "I wish you would visit me at the United States Hotel, and bring your wife with you. I could tell her about her mother, and if you want to send letters to Georgia, I will take them for you."

Later that day, a porter from the hotel delivered a poorly spelled note to William at the furniture store:

Oct. 22 1850
Wm Craft, Sir—I have to leave Eirley in the morning....If you want me to carry a letter home with me, you must bring it to the United States Hotel....If your wif wants to se me you could bring her with you....

John Knight

P.S. I shall leave for home eirley Thursday morning [October 24]. J.K.

William asked the messenger if Mr. Knight was alone at the hotel. No, he was told. A short, sandy-haired man was with him—a Mr. Hughes. William shuddered, for Knight's companion was undoubtedly Willis Hughes, the Macon town jailer. William and Ellen's owners had apparently sent Knight and Hughes to Boston to reclaim them through the courts if they could or by force if necessary.

Knight did not leave on Thursday morning as he had said in his note. Instead, he and Hughes remained in Boston, trying to find a court that would order the arrest of the Crafts under the Fugitive Slave Law, while looking for an opportunity to seize the couple. Willis Hughes was heard to brag, "I am the jailer at Macon. I catch Negoes sometimes. I am here for William and Ellen Craft and, damn 'em, I will have them if I stay till eternity. And if there are not men enough in Massachusetts to take them I will bring them from the South. It is not the niggers I care for—it is the principle of the thing!"

It was the "principle of the thing" to Boston's abolitionists, too, only they believed there was a higher law than the Fugitive Slave Law. Black Bostonians expressed this at a meeting when they passed a resolution declaring, "Man wills us slaves, but God wills us free. God's will be done!"

As in Revolutionary days, hundreds of Bostonians armed themselves, but now the slave hunters rather than the English were the enemies. Abolitionists escorted William and Ellen to work and stood guard outside their boarding house. Posters proclaiming "Slave hunters in Boston! Shall these villains remain here?" were nailed to trees and placed in windows around the city. Wherever Knight and Hughes went, they were followed by groups of children who yelled at them, "Slave hunters! There go the slave hunters! Go back to Georgia!" And *The Liberator* reported that "two prowling villains" were searching the city for the Crafts.

Although greatly outnumbered, Knight and Hughes had the law of the United States on their side. The two slave hunters asked a federal court in Boston to issue a warrant for the Crafts' arrest. The couple was charged with having stolen themselves and their clothing from their owners. Under the Fugitive Slave Law's provisions, the court had no choice but to issue the warrant, yet for a time the government made no attempt to arrest the Georgia Fugitives.

Boston's abolitionists struck back with their own legal maneuvers, harassing Knight and Hughes at every turn. On Saturday, October 26, Knight and Hughes were arrested for slandering William Craft by calling him a slave. They had to post bail to avoid jail. On Monday, October 28, the two men from Macon were arrested for plotting to kidnap Ellen and William Craft. Once again Knight and Hughes had to post bail. Willis Hughes later told the *Federal Union* newspaper of Milledgeville (which was then the capital of Georgia) that while in the Boston area he was also arrested "for smoking in the streets, for swearing in the streets, for carrying concealed weapons, for driving fast through the streets, and for passing Cambridge Bridge without paying the toll (which was not true)."

Children yelled at them, "Slave hunters! There go the slave hunters! Go back to Georgia!"

The entire nation was following the "Craft case," for it was a test of whether the Fugitive Slave Law would be enforced or not. To resolve the dilemma, a wealthy Bostonian offered to buy William and Ellen from their owners, no matter what the cost. The slave catchers could then go home and the Crafts could live in peace. But Ellen and William Craft rejected the offer, for it would not help the thousands of other runaway slaves.

"We represent all the fugitive slaves," William said at a meeting. "Ellen and I would not want our freedom bought if it could be purchased for two cents!" William was also overheard to tell Frederick Douglass, "Our people have been pursued long enough. If we can't live here and be free, we will die!"

One day a mob of abolitionists surrounded Willis Hughes when he was stepping into a carriage. Suddenly a Bostonian pulled a gun and tried to shoot him. The Reverend Theodore Parker grabbed the gunman at the last moment, saving Hughes's life.

"I will not let you have his murder on your conscience!" Reverend Parker told the would-be killer.

Soon after, at 6 A.M. on the morning of Wednesday, October 30, Reverend Parker and about 20 other members of the Committee of Safety and Vigilance went to the United States Hotel to speak to Willis Hughes and John Knight. The abolitionist minister advised them to leave town.

"We came here to execute the law," Hughes protested.

"Yes, but you must be satisfied that you cannot arrest William and Ellen Craft, and if you do, you cannot carry them out of the city," Reverend Parker responded. "I have stood between you and violence once. I do not promise to do it again!"

Reverend Theodore Parker was so staunchly anti-slavery that he was eager for a war to free the slaves.

Perhaps Hughes and Knight now had an inkling of how the Crafts had felt upon fleeing Macon. They followed Reverend Parker's advice, but the Bostonians were so infuriated at them that they had to sneak out of the city. The two men went to a town outside Boston where they caught a train that took them to safety.

But those who wanted to capture the Crafts didn't give up. Georgia newspapers published articles by John Knight and Willis Hughes complaining about their treatment in Boston. In his November 13 article in the *Georgia Journal and Messenger* of Macon, Knight wrote that many Bostonians supported the Fugitive Slave Law but were quiet about it. Judging by the spelling in his October 22 note to William Craft, someone must have helped Knight write this article.

"The abolitionists and negroes are very numerous, and apparently have things very much their own way at present," Knight admitted, but "the business men, and men of property, said that the law ought to be executed, and that if it came to a trial of strength, the negroes and abolitionists would be put down."

Hughes bitterly complained in the November 26 Milledgeville *Federal Union* that authorities in Boston had gone to great lengths to insure the safety of British abolitionist lecturer George Thompson when he came to visit. Meanwhile, they hadn't done a thing to protect Hughes:

> *In reference to the abolition sentiment in Boston, I would state this circumstance. All the time the excitement was going on with me, there was no protection of the city authorities offered me, and none turned out in my favor. But when George Thompson, the English abolition Lecturer was expected, and a meeting was announced to receive him, it was rumored that a mob might assemble on his reception, and the Mayor instantly ordered out the city officers to attend and suppress any mob—showing that the city authorities were disposed to give protection to an abolitionist, which they had withheld from me while engaged in my lawful business; and my opinion is, if we had succeeded in arresting the negroes, that they would have been rescued by the citizens. I will conclude by saying that I went to Boston as an agent to execute a lawful trust, thinking I should be protected and assisted by the laws of my country. But on the contrary, from the first, the laws of the country, instead of proving a protection, were made an engine of cruelty, oppression, injustice, and abuse, so that my life was constantly endangered, and this without the first offer of assistance from Government, national, State, or city. I feel that every man who has a Southern heart in his bosom, and would maintain the honor of his country, should sustain the Southern Rights Cause, by every Constitutional measure, until our rights are acknowledged and Justice obtained.*
>
> *Willis H. Hughes*

On November 2, Ellen's former master, Dr. Robert Collins, wrote to President Fillmore demanding that he enforce the Fugitive Slave Law. The situation was too explosive for him to become involved, President Fillmore responded through an aide. "The President feels the importance of avoiding, as far as practicable, all causes of irritation between the North and the

South," the aide wrote, "and especially on the exciting subject of Slavery." Nonetheless, rumors swept Boston that the President was going to enforce the Fugitive Slave Law by sending in hundreds of soldiers to capture the Crafts. Were that to happen, there could be fighting in the streets of Boston.

Their friends decided that in order to avoid an armed clash in Boston, and for the Crafts' own safety, the couple should go into hiding. For a time they stayed at the homes of abolitionists in the Boston area. Reverend Theodore Parker and his wife, Lydia, hid Ellen for a few days in an upstairs room of their home. On November 6, 1850, Reverend Parker wrote in his journal:

> *Ellen Craft has been here all the week since Monday; went off at a quarter past six to-night. That is a pretty state of things, that I am liable to be fined 1000 dollars and jailed for six months for sheltering one of my own parishioners, who has violated no law of God, and only took possession of herself! Talk in the newspapers about the President sending on 600 or 700 soldiers to dragoon us into keeping the Fugitive Slave Law!*

William, meanwhile, was staying at Lewis and Harriet Hayden's boarding-house. In his basement, Hayden had stashed two kegs of gunpowder. He threatened to blow up his house rather than surrender William to authorities.

Ellen and William felt that, in a way, they had already been re-enslaved, for they couldn't be together, go to work, or even show their faces around town. Every time there was a knock at the door or a shadow on the wall, they thought it was Willis Hughes, John Knight, or any of a thousand other slave catchers come to grab them. As Ellen slept, she dreamed that they were being chased by slave hunters. Besides worrying constantly about danger to themselves, the Crafts suffered from knowing that those who sheltered them could be heavily fined and sent to jail. The couple reached a sad conclusion: The time had come for them to leave Boston.

There was no longer any place in the United States where Ellen and William could live, for slave hunters could now pursue them wherever they settled on American soil. Not even in Canada, where many other fugitives had found a safe haven, would the couple be safe. Because of their fame, the Crafts made inviting targets for the slave hunters who occasionally defied

British law and tried to kidnap escaped slaves living in Canada. Visiting British abolitionist George Thompson convinced the Crafts that they could find freedom and peace only if they sailed across the Atlantic Ocean and settled in England.

Before leaving Boston, there was something Ellen and William wanted to do. They had always craved a wedding service performed by a minister. Reverend Theodore Parker agreed to perform the ceremony. On the morning of November 7, 1850, William and Ellen were escorted

The Georgia Telegraph

MACON, GA., TUESDAY MORNING, NOVEMBER 19, 1850

"Oh, take your time Miss Lucy."

On Friday the 8th inst., William Crafts and Ellen Crafts, the fugitive slaves from this city, about which all New England has been agog for the last three weeks, were married in Boston, by the Rev. Theodore Parker, and left for England via Halifax, in contempt of the officers and law of the United States, after successfully defying them for about two weeks.

On the *evening of the same day*, we learn, says the *Southern Press*, that the Democrats, and on the *next day* the Whigs of Boston, held meetings and resolved that while the Fugitive slave law remained the law of the land it should be maintained. The Whigs, however, resolved that it should be modified.

It is known to our city readers, that Mr. Knight, one of the agents employed by the owners of these slaves to go to Boston and aid in their arrest, has already returned to Macon. As we write we learn that Mr. Hughes, the other gentleman employed, is on his way home. Thus ends another act of this fugitive slave bill farce. Who will say now that the Compromise bill does not work like a charm?

A re-creation of the 1850 Georgia Telegraph *article announcing the Crafts' marriage.*

from their hiding places to their apartment at the Haydens' boardinghouse. While friends guarded the building, Reverend Parker performed the marriage on that Thursday morning.

Parker never performed another wedding like the Crafts'. At the end of the ceremony, he gave the couple a Bible and a long-bladed weapon called a bowie knife. The Bible could save their souls, he said, while the knife could save their lives.

"I hate violence," said Reverend Parker. "I reverence the sacredness of human life, and think there is seldom a case in which it is justifiable to take it. But if you can save your wife's liberty in no other way, William, then this is one of those cases!" Reverend Parker concluded the ceremony with a prayer asking that the couple be granted a future as pleasant as their former lives had been difficult.

CHAPTER SIX

FUGITIVES AGAIN

The bride and groom had no time for a honeymoon. Immediately after the wedding they said farewell to the many friends whom they had grown to love during their two years in Boston. Then the newlyweds set off on a new journey.

The couple could have traveled by steamship directly from Boston to Liverpool, England. However, Ellen and William's friends feared that slave catchers might try to kidnap the couple at the Boston docks. They arranged for them to travel secretly to Portland, Maine, more than 100 miles to the north, where they were to board a steamship for England. Everyone was so secretive about the Crafts' route to Portland that the details remain unknown to this day.

Upon arriving in Portland, Ellen and William learned some distressing news. The steamer they planned to take to England had collided with another vessel the previous night and was out of commission. To catch a steamship bound for England, they would have to continue farther on to the city of Halifax, Nova Scotia, in Canada.

From Portland, the Crafts took a steamer up the coast of Maine to Saint John, New Brunswick, 50 miles beyond the United States border. They spent two days in Saint John, then boarded another steamer that carried them to Windsor, on the finger-shaped peninsula of Nova Scotia. As they boarded a stagecoach at Windsor for the 50-mile ride to Halifax, the Crafts

An ocean-going steamship similar to the one that transported the Crafts to England in port in the mid-1800s.

discovered that outlawing slavery didn't mean that Canada had overcome prejudice. "I won't have a nigger riding inside with white folks," the driver told William. He had to sit on the outside of the vehicle next to the driver, even though it was pouring rain.

They were just seven miles from Halifax when the coach suddenly skidded in the mud and overturned. William fell on the driver and had to pull the man's head out of the mud to prevent him from suffocating. Seconds later, Ellen and the other passengers climbed out of the vehicle. Although bruised, scratched, and covered with mud, the passengers had no serious injuries. Over the next several hours they slogged through the rain to Halifax, arriving after nightfall.

Once again bad luck dogged them. Because of the stagecoach accident, the Crafts had reached Halifax too late. The steamship had left for England two hours earlier. They would have to wait two weeks in Halifax for the next vessel.

The couple walked with the other disappointed travelers to an inn. Suspecting that the landlady wouldn't rent them a room if she saw him, William stood outside in a downpour while Ellen paid for lodgings for herself and her husband. The landlady assumed that Ellen was white and accepted her money. But when William began to carry their luggage inside, the landlady rushed to Ellen's room and rapped on the door.

"Do you know the dark man downstairs?" the landlady asked Ellen.

"Yes, he is my husband," she answered.

"I mean the black man—the nigger!"

"I quite understand you—he is my husband!" Ellen repeated.

"My God!" the landlady exclaimed, storming out of the room.

The next morning the landlady knocked on the door again. Her other guests had been complaining, the landlady explained. Several had threatened to leave unless the Crafts were evicted. "I think you had better go," the landlady ordered. "You must understand, I have no prejudice myself, but if you stop here we shall lose all our customers."

Ellen and William hadn't felt well when they left Boston. By this time, they had very bad colds from having walked seven miles in the storm. Nonetheless, the landlady made them leave.

The couple had trouble finding another place to stay, for no white innkeepers would rent to them. Finally, they were directed to a black couple, the

Reverend and Mrs. Cannady, who put them up for two weeks, charging only a little rent. The Cannadys also arranged for a doctor to care for them. With antibiotics nearly a hundred years in the future, even the best physicians couldn't do much to combat infection in 1850. By the time their steamship, the *Cambria,* approached Halifax in late November, Ellen was feeling even worse.

When he went to the steamship office to purchase tickets, William encountered a new problem. Tickets weren't sold until the vessel was ready to depart, the ticket agent told him. William discovered that this wasn't true, so he returned to the office and again asked to buy two tickets to Liverpool, England. "The vessel is full and you had better try to get to Liverpool by other means," the ticket agent said. William knew that the steamship company was refusing to sell him tickets because he was black. Fortunately, during their stay in Halifax, William had become friends with a white abolitionist. This man went with him to the steamship office, and the agent reluctantly sold two tickets to Liverpool, England, to William Craft.

By the time the *Cambria* headed out to sea, Ellen was terribly ill, suffering from chills, fever, and a painful cough. She had developed pneumonia, a lung disease that killed about half its victims in the 1800s. Ellen grew so weak that William was afraid she would not survive the 3,000-mile ocean crossing. But toward the end of the three-week voyage, her condition improved. When the coast of England came into view, she managed to dress and come out on deck with William to view their new homeland.

The next day, about a week before Christmas of 1850, the *Cambria* docked in Liverpool, England. It was nearly two years to the day since Ellen and William Craft had left their little cabin in Macon, Georgia.

They had traveled 5,000 miles and were free at last.

CHAPTER SEVEN

A NEW LIFE in ENGLAND

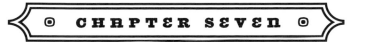

The Crafts faced a new set of problems in England. Ellen was still weak from her bout with pneumonia. They had little money, no home or job prospects, and they were strangers in a country thousands of miles from their birthplace. Yet they rejoiced to step onto English soil, for they were finally beyond the grasp of the slave hunters.

Ironically, the English city where the Crafts landed had become prosperous from the slave trade. Over many years, half the three million African slaves taken across the Atlantic to the New World by the British had been transported in ships out of Liverpool. During the late 1700s and the early 1800s alone, three quarters of all European slaving ships had departed from Liverpool.

For a few days, Ellen and William lodged at a Liverpool hotel. As the news spread that the Georgia Fugitives were in the city, a minister and his wife invited them into their home. Under their kind care, Ellen gradually regained her strength.

It happened that an old friend of the Crafts was in England. William Wells Brown had come to Europe to speak about world peace and the evils of slavery. Always bursting with enthusiasm and new ideas, Brown met with the Crafts and proposed a plan. Thousands of people in England and Scotland, he explained, had fought to end slavery in their countries and wanted it outlawed everywhere. Many of these people had heard about

A view of the backyards of London rowhouses at about the time Ellen and William arrived.

the Crafts and would pay to see them. William and Ellen accepted Brown's offer to organize a speaking tour similar to their earlier trip through New England. As before, the tour would raise money for the abolitionist movement and for the Crafts.

Brown hired a London artist to paint a gigantic canvas diorama showing 24 scenes from slave life in America. This movable canvas became the backdrop for a theatrical production about slavery that Brown created. He and the Crafts then began their tour. In each town they visited, they rented a theater or lecture hall where they set up their diorama. The three ex-slaves then posted signs around town advertising their show.

Their presentations drew large crowds. Standing in front of the diorama, Brown would describe the horrors of slave life. "The name of the United States is hissed in every clime," Brown would tell the audience. "My country is indeed the land of oppression. There is not a territory over which the Stars and Stripes flies, on which William and Ellen Craft, or myself, could be protected by law. Wherever the American flag is seen flying on the continent of the New World, it points to us as slaves. We enjoy tonight a degree of freedom in your town that we could not, if we were in the land of our birth!"

Next would come the highlight of the show. The Georgia Fugitives would step forward and Ellen would model her disguise as her husband described their long journey to England. The story of their years as slaves moved audiences to tears, while the account of their escape always drew cheers and applause. William also asked his audience to do something to combat slavery. He requested

A portrait of Ellen Craft dressed as Mr. Johnson from the Illustrated London News.

FUGITIVES FROM SLAVERY.—REMARKABLE

RETURN IN THE CENSUS.

We are reminded by Mr. Russell's powerful denunciation of Slavery of a remarkable instance of its baneful effects, which has just been illustrated by means of the census return in Yorkshire. It appears that William and Ellen Craft have lately been relating, at the Woodhouse Mechanics' Institute, a touching account of their escape from slavery; and as they sojourned with Mr. Wilson Armistead, of Leeds, on the 30th of March, it was requisite that their names and places of nativity, as well as their rank and profession, should be inserted by him in the Government Census paper to be filled up and returned on the 31st. These two individuals were accordingly entered by Mr. Armistead under their real designation "Fugitives from Slavery in America, the land of their nativity!" This is a startling entry, perhaps more extraordinary than any in the new return of our population.

The particulars of the escape of these fugitives from slavery are of the most romantic character. William and Ellen Craft were reared in Georgia, under different masters; but, living near to each other they became eventually man and wife. William is a black man, but his wife Ellen is nearly white. Whenever they met, after their marriage, they contrived and discussed plan of escape, and in 1848 this was accomplished; the wife, with her hair cut off, and wearing green spectacles, disguised herself as a young man, and her husband as her slave or servant. They first travelled to Savannah, and then took the steamboat to Charleston, in Carolina. After escaping many dangers of betrayal, and having now expended their savings in obtaining their liberty, they settled in Boston, William to work at his trade of cabinet-making, and Ellen to work with her needle. In this way they maintained themselves, learned to read and write at evening schools, until the Fugitive Slave-law came into operation, and on the very first evening they attended the school the warrant was issued for their apprehension, and the slave-catchers were abroad in Boston. The excitement and agitation of the three or four day's hunt in Boston were extreme; but William and Ellen ultimately succeeded in getting on board a British vessel, while the kidnappers were at New York.

The fugitives arrived about four months since in Liverpool, where, for the first time, they set foot on really free soil. They are very interesting and intelligent persons. Ellen is twenty-four years of age, and as fair as most of her British sisters. William is very dark, but of a reflective, intelligent countenance.

A re-creation of an article published in the Illustrated London News *of April 19, 1851, along with the picture of Ellen in her costume that appears on the page 66.*

that English people avoid buying goods produced by American slaves, especially rice, sugar, and cotton. By putting money in the pockets of plantation owners, he explained, they helped support the institution of slavery. In fact, he figured, by purchasing such slave-produced items, every seven British families indirectly enslaved one person.

Sometimes William Craft appeared alone, especially when Ellen was recovering from her illness. Although audiences were disappointed at not seeing her, William gave some noteworthy talks on his own. One speech that he made at a church in Edinburgh, Scotland, on December 30, 1850, was reported a month later in the *National Anti-Slavery Standard* in New York City:

It affords me great pleasure to meet with you here this evening, not because I feel capable of interesting you with a speech, but because I feel myself in the midst of friends, amongst whom I can exclaim, Thank God, I am free! It is only two years since I escaped from slavery, and previous to my escape I was unable to read a syllable. My wife and I escaped together from Georgia, and came on to Boston. We remained quietly in Boston for about two years, till the passage of the Fugitive Slave Bill....We were compelled in the end to flee to a country where we could feel ourselves in greater security.

In Bristol, England, the Crafts became friends with John Estlin, an abolitionist physician. Dr. Estlin invited the couple to stay in his home. He also arranged for the three ex-slaves to speak at a number of places in England and Wales, which along with Scotland and Ireland comprised Great Britain.

Portrait of Ellen Craft

Before long, the Crafts were celebrities in Britain. British newspapers and magazines published numerous stories about the couple. For example, the *Illustrated London News* ran a feature about them, accompanied by a drawing of Ellen in her disguise. Some of Britain's most influential people clamored to meet the Crafts. In the mountainous Lake District of northwest England they met Harriet Martineau, a fiery abolitionist and feminist who had attacked slavery in her book, *Society in America.* Miss Martineau, who was nearly deaf, listened to Ellen's story through an ear trumpet. After Ellen finished, Miss Martineau angrily said: "I wish every woman in the British Empire could hear that tale as I have, so they might know how their own sex was treated in that boasted land of liberty."

In Dundee, Scotland, Ellen and William met astronomer Thomas Dick, who showed them the stars and planets through his telescope. Elsewhere on their tour they visited castles and churches, museums and libraries, and met such distinguished people as Alfred, Lord Tennyson, who was Great Britain's poet laureate, and Lady Noel Byron, who was the widow of poet Lord Byron.

In the spring of 1851, the Crafts attended the first world's fair, the Great Exhibition, which was held in a huge glass building called the Crystal Palace in London. On the Saturday that the Crafts visited the fair, Great Britain's Queen Victoria and her Royal Family also attended, along with members of the British Parliament. The Crafts may have been introduced to the queen and her husband, Prince Albert, who was president of the British Anti-Slavery Society.

Meeting prominent people did not go to the Crafts' heads. On the contrary, it made them keenly aware that they had been prevented from achieving anything noteworthy except for their escape from slavery, and that they couldn't even read very well. While gazing through Thomas Dick's telescope, they were filled with questions about the universe, but the books on his shelves might as well have been written in hieroglyphics as far as they were concerned. When people spoke about Lady Byron's late husband, the Crafts wanted to read his poems, but they weren't able to do so.

Portrait of William Craft

After a few months, the Georgia Fugitives decided to retire from their speaking tour and continue the education they had begun on the Ivens farm outside Philadelphia. Thanks to Lady Byron and Dr. Estlin, their wish was fulfilled.

Lady Byron's daughter, Lady Lovelace, had begun a school in Ockham, a village 20 miles outside London. The students at Ockham School studied reading, writing, arithmetic, and geography and also learned what were called "industrial skills" such as sewing, carpentry, and farming. Lady Byron and Dr. Estlin raised funds to send the Crafts to Ockham School and to provide them with a small cottage nearby. Now 28 and 25 years old, William and Ellen became the school's oldest but most eager students. Early each morning they walked up School Lane to class. Soon they were reading the poems and science books that had been beyond their grasp a few months earlier. In the afternoon, the couple taught in the school. William conducted the boys' carpentry class while Ellen ran the girls' sewing class.

Now that they could write, the Crafts sent letters to friends in the United States describing their new lives. They asked one friend to excuse them for not communicating earlier because "we have been deprived of the art of writing. As writing becomes more easy to us, we will take great pleasure in sending you a few lines from time to time." No one ever had a better excuse for not writing sooner. They simply hadn't known how!

Their life at Ockham was the most peaceful period the Crafts had ever known. Confident that they were truly free, the couple decided to begin the family they had long delayed. On October 22, 1852, Ellen gave birth to a son. The new parents named their baby Charles Estlin Phillips Craft, after friends on two continents, Dr. Estlin and Wendell Phillips. William proudly wrote to a friend in Boston, "I know that you and other friends will heartily rejoice to learn that my wife has given birth to our first free born babe, on the 22nd of October, and I am more than thankful to say that both he and his dear mother are now doing well."

Meanwhile, word reached the Crafts that an ugly rumor about Ellen was circulating through the United States, particularly in the South. Because she was homesick and not happy with being free, the gossipers claimed, Ellen had made a deal with a white Southerner who was visiting London. She would voluntarily become this man's slave if he would take her back to Georgia! Ellen was so enraged by this rumor that on October 26, 1852—just four days after giving birth—she fired off an angry letter to the *Anti-Slavery Advocate* in London. That December the *Anti-Slavery Advocate,* which the Crafts' friend Dr. Estlin edited, published Ellen's scathing response to the gossip:

Ockham School, Oct 26, 1852

Dear Sir:

I feel very much obliged to you for informing me of the erroneous report which has been extensively circulated in the American newspapers: "That I had placed myself in the hands of an American gentleman in London, on condition that he would take me back to the family who held me as a slave in Georgia." I write these few lines to say that the statement is entirely unfounded, for I never had the slightest inclination of returning to bondage; and God forbid that I should be so false to liberty as to prefer slavery in its stead. In fact, since my escape from slavery, I have got on much better in every respect than I could have possibly anticipated. Though, had it been to the contrary, my feelings in regard to this would have been just the same, for I had much rather starve in England, a free woman, than be a slave for the best man that ever breathed upon the American continent.

Yours very truly,
Ellen Craft

The Crafts had been at Ockham School for two years when they were offered paying jobs there—William as superintendent of the school's industrial department and Ellen as supervisor of girls. The couple carefully weighed this proposition before informing the school's directors of their decision: They appreciated the offer but were turning it down. When asked why, they explained that they wanted to open a boardinghouse in London. The truth was, while they were grateful for all the help from their abolitionist friends, they felt that these well-meaning people wanted to control their lives. William and Ellen were eager to go out into the world on their own and see what they could accomplish without any help.

Their decision caused quite a stir. England was much less race conscious, but far more class conscious, than the United States. For several years the Crafts had been taking tea and attending parties with the "upper class" and "intellectual elite"—lords and ladies, poets and novelists, ministers and teachers. Their English friends were astonished that they would choose to abandon this life and run a boardinghouse like common people.

Dr. Estlin tried to talk the Crafts out of their plan and became irritated at William for not following his advice. William was "selfwilled," Dr. Estlin wrote, and "must go through this necessary business of burning his fingers," meaning failing with the boardinghouse, before returning to his friends for help. Another abolitionist accused William of pushing Ellen to a decision that she knew was foolish. "He is so proud and secretive that it is difficult for Dr. Estlin to advise him," wrote this acquaintance, "and Ellen defers so entirely to him that her natural good sense is lost in his folly."

Actually, Ellen wanted her little family to strike out on its own, too. She was weary of telling and retelling the story of their escape to the many visitors who came to their cottage, and she despised having to dress in her costume for every prominent abolitionist who was curious to see it. Besides, she had begun to feel that she and William had become the pets of the abolitionists, who enjoyed showing off how well the ex-slaves had learned to read and write.

One day in 1853, Ellen and William packed their belongings, said good-bye to the students and staff of Ockham School, and departed from their cottage with their year-old son. They moved only 20 miles away into London, but to the Crafts it was almost like being on another planet. Ockham was a quiet, green village of 200 people. London was the world's largest city, a place of crowded slums and smoky factories, a metropolis where more people lived on a single block than inhabited all of Ockham, and where speeding carriages made crossing the streets a challenge.

As they had planned, they opened a lodging house. Dr. Estlin proved to be partly right and partly wrong. The Crafts' boardinghouse soon went out of business, but they refused to turn to their former protectors for help. Instead they tried other kinds of work so that they could continue living on their own.

They began a business in which they sold raincoats and other rubber goods. They also wrote *Running a Thousand Miles for Freedom,* a book about their escape from bondage. It was published in London in 1860, but copies reached the United States, where it awakened many readers to the evils of slavery. A drawing of Ellen in her disguise that appeared at the front of the book became so popular that the Crafts added to their income by selling copies of it. Ellen and William also resumed lecturing. Despite her distaste for displaying her costume, Ellen earned a reputation for being an effective anti-slavery speaker.

The Crafts needed to earn all the money they could because their family was growing. A second son, William Jr., was born to the couple in 1855. Later came another son, Brougham; a daughter, named Ellen for her mother; and a boy named Alfred.

Their lecturing and other enterprises enabled William and Ellen to buy a home in Hammersmith, a London suburb. They raised their own children in this cottage, as well as three adopted African boys who entered their lives in an unusual way.

In 1862 a group of British merchants asked William Craft to deliver a cargo of trade goods to the Kingdom of Dahomey (now Benin) on Africa's west coast. William was to exchange

RUNNING A THOUSAND MILES

FOR FREEDOM

OR, THE ESCAPE

OF

WILLIAM AND ELLEN CRAFT

FROM SLAVERY.

" Slaves cannot breathe in England : if their lungs
Receive our air, that moment they are free ;
They touch our country, and their shackles fall."
COWPER.

LONDON:
WILLIAM TWEEDIE, 337, STRAND.
——
1860.

The title page of the Crafts' book
Running a Thousand Miles for Freedom.

the merchandise for palm oil, which the English prized for its use in skin cream and medicine. His mission was to have a second purpose. British abolitionists wanted William to persuade the king of Dahomey to stop selling captured Africans as slaves, for this practice contributed to the continuation of slavery.

William was hesitant to leave his wife and children, but the abolitionists convinced him that it would be a great achievement if he could talk the king into ending the slave trade. William also had another reason for making this voyage. His family's roots were in west Africa. Decades earlier, his grandparents had been kidnapped into slavery from Africa's west coast, where his grandfather had been a tribal chief. William left his wife and children in their cottage in Hammersmith and sailed to the land of his ancestors.

He later referred to his trip in a talk he gave in Newcastle upon Tyne, England, in August 1863, but details about the expedition are scanty. Apparently William's dark skin, which had been such a handicap in the United States, was greatly admired in Africa. It also appears that the king of Dahomey liked him. After lengthy but friendly negotiations, William traded his merchandise for a huge cargo of palm oil and other African goods. However, William was bitterly disappointed by his inability to convince the king to end the slave trade. In fact, the king gave him three African slave boys as a gift.

William boarded the ship with the boys and in 1863 sailed back to his wife and children. We can only imagine their astonishment at meeting the African boys and hearing how they had been given to William. Ellen and William freed the boys and welcomed them into their home as their adopted sons. Ellen taught the boys to read and write.

About a year after returning home, William was asked to make a second trip to Africa. The merchants were eager for more African goods, while the abolitionists hoped that, with a little more prodding, the king would stop selling slaves. Once again William reluctantly parted from his family, and in early November 1864, he sailed from England to the west coast of Africa.

The king greeted William like an old friend. He built a little house for him, accepted his trade goods, and agreed to consider ending the slave trade. William expected to be paid for his merchandise with palm oil and other African goods as in the past, but when he prepared to sail home, he received the shock of his life. The king paid for the merchandise by delivering 60 slaves, chained to one another, to William.

One of the world's most famous
ex-slaves suddenly found himself
in the strange position of
owning 60 human beings.

One of the world's most famous ex-slaves suddenly found himself in the strange position of owning 60 human beings. William's first inclination was to return the slaves to the king, but he would just sell them to someone else.

The more William thought about it, the clearer it became that he had been presented with a wonderful opportunity. He took the slaves aboard his ship and transported them to a British colony in Africa, where he set them free. William Craft then returned to England, reaching home about two and a half years after his second departure.

The merchants were displeased when William returned empty-handed, for the trading mission had cost them a fortune. They paid William very little for his second trip to Dahomey. Still, he had the satisfaction of knowing that, somewhere in Africa, 60 people were free thanks to him.

Meanwhile, Ellen and William had been trying to free their own relatives. For a price, slaves could often be bought out of bondage. There were many instances of runaway slaves and other free blacks saving money for years to buy a wife, husband, child, or parent. Generally the price was steep—a thousand dollars or more (equivalent to at least $20,000 today)—because the slave owners knew that the buyers were desperate to free their loved ones. Soon after learning to write, the Crafts had sent letters to Georgia trying to find their relatives and purchase their freedom. William tracked down his mother and bought her out of slavery. Haunted still by the memory of his sister Sarah being led away in a cart, he discovered that she was living in Mississippi. He purchased Sarah's freedom, too, and saw to it that she and their mother were reunited. But the Smith family was so angry over Ellen's escape that they absolutely refused to sell her mother, Maria, for any amount of money. Maria had to remain a slave until something occurred that forced her owners to liberate her.

A war over slavery broke out between the North and the South in 1861. At that time, Northerners called it the War of Southern Rebellion, while to Southerners it was the War of Northern Aggression. What we today call the Civil War cost more American lives than any other conflict in United States history. More than 620,000 soldiers died. In 1865 the North won the Civil War, liberating the remaining Southern slaves. Once Maria was free, Ellen sent her money so that she could come to England.

Leaving Macon, Georgia, Maria embarked on her own long journey. She sailed across the ocean to England and then boarded a train for London. On a November day in 1865, while William was away on his second trip to Dahomey, Ellen took her children to a London train station. For a moment

Ellen and the middle-aged woman who stepped off the train stared at one another. Then the mother and daughter embraced for the first time in 17 years. Maria moved into the cottage at Hammersmith and helped care for the grandchildren she had never before seen.

With her mother there to help, Ellen became more involved in causes that were dear to her. She sewed clothing, which she sent to the newly freed black people in the South. She raised funds to aid the American ex-slaves and to build schools in Africa. Ellen also protested injustice whenever she could.

One night at a dinner party, Ellen was seated next to Edward Eyre, former governor of the British-ruled island of Jamaica. Eyre had ruthlessly put down a rebellion of black Jamaicans, executing black lawmaker George Gordon. Ellen ripped into Eyre angrily and demanded, "Do you not yourself now feel that poor Gordon was unjustly executed?" At a loss for words, Eyre rose from the table and didn't return.

At another gathering Ellen was introduced to Artemus Ward, an American humorist who made fun of black people in his stories and lectures. "They tell me that you are always very hard upon the poor Negro," Ellen said.

Photographs like this one of dead soldiers showed people the horrors of the Civil War.

Ward denied it, but Ellen wouldn't let him off so easily. She looked at him icily and said, "I hope you will never again write anything which shall make people believe that you are against the Negro." Whether Ward would have taken Ellen Craft's advice is unknown, for he died soon after, in early 1867.

When William returned to his family in the spring of 1867, Ellen was proud to hear how he had freed the 60 Africans. She also knew that the time had come for them to make a decision. To their children, England was home and America just a far-off place where their parents had been slaves long ago. But with slavery ended, Ellen and William yearned to return to the nation of their birth. Besides, people who could educate the ex-slaves were desperately needed in America.

On January 1, 1863, President Lincoln issued the Emancipation Proclamation, paving the way for freeing the slaves.

Ellen and William discussed the move with their family. Everyone was agreeable except their sons William Jr. and Brougham, 14 and 12 years old, respectively. The two boys wanted to remain in England to complete their schooling. Their parents granted this wish, arranging for the boys to live with friends. The three African boys may have remained in England to complete their education before returning to Africa as teachers.

In the summer of 1869 Ellen and William sold their cottage in Hammersmith and said farewell to their many English friends. Then, accompanied by three of their children and Ellen's mother, Maria, they left their home in England. The family traveled by train to Liverpool, the city where Ellen and William had first landed 19 years earlier. In Liverpool the Crafts boarded a steamer and were soon at sea, headed for home.

CHAPTER EIGHT

GOING
HOME

The Crafts were going home, but the question was: Exactly where *was* home? Now that they could live wherever they chose, Ellen and William considered the possibilities. Should they settle in Boston, where people had defended them from slave hunters, or in Philadelphia, where they had first tasted freedom? Or should they return to their birthplace, Georgia, where they had so many ties but so many heart-breaking memories?

Their first stop was Boston, where once again they moved in with Lewis and Harriet Hayden, the couple who had sheltered them 20 years earlier. They remained with the Haydens for more than six months. Old friends came to visit Ellen and William and to meet the three children who had come to the United States with them: 17-year-old Charles, 8-year-old Ellen, and the new baby, Alfred. Journalists who interviewed them were impressed by the black family that had the manners and speech of English aristocrats.

The Crafts had returned to the United States during a period of great hope for the nation's black people. In early 1870 the 15th Amendment to the federal Constitution had been ratified, guaranteeing African Americans their voting rights. William and Ellen attended meetings with old Boston abolitionists to celebrate the passage of the amendment. William was also invited to speak at gatherings about his experiences in Africa.

Four generations of an African American family enjoying freedom after their emancipation from slavery.

A freedmen's school in Richmond, Virginia. Freed slaves of all ages learned to read and write in such schools.

For several years following the Civil War, the United States stationed soldiers in the South to protect black people from the former slave owners. Black southern men began to vote (a right which was denied American women regardless of color) and to win public office. In 1870 Joseph H. Rainey of South Carolina became the first black member of the U.S. House of Representatives and Hiram Rhodes Revels of Mississippi became the first black U.S. Senator. The federal government also created a special agency to assist the "freedmen," as the ex-slaves were known. Called the Freedmen's Bureau, this agency helped the freedmen establish their own farms and businesses and opened thousands of schools for black Southerners.

A writer from the Boston area helped make the Crafts' story familiar to the students at the freedmen's schools. In 1826, Lydia Maria Child had founded the *Juvenile Miscellany,* the country's first monthly children's magazine. The year the Freedmen's Bureau was founded—1865—Child compiled *The Freedmen's Book.* This textbook for the freedmen's schools contained essays, poems, and short biographies of noteworthy African Americans. The chapter on the Crafts chronicled their escape from slavery and their later life up to the year 1864.

In the 1870s the Freedmen's Bureau was disbanded and the federal troops were gradually withdrawn from the South. With the federal government out of the picture, white Southerners devised ways to deprive the former slaves of the rights they had briefly enjoyed. They closed down black schools and passed state laws preventing black citizens from voting or holding public office. The Ku Klux Klan and other hate groups beat up or murdered blacks who tried to vote or compete with whites for jobs. The American justice system was also closed off to the freedmen, for Southern blacks weren't allowed to serve on juries or testify in court. Instead of receiving a fair trial as guaranteed by the Bill of Rights, blacks accused of crimes were often lynched—seized by mobs and murdered.

Deprived of educational and job opportunities, most blacks went back to work for their former owners. They were paid low wages and treated much like they had been in the days of slavery, as white Southerners re-established control over their states.

Ellen and William Craft decided to help their people. Early in 1870 they announced their intention to visit relatives in Macon and then start a school for black people somewhere nearby. Sixty-eight-year-old Lydia Maria Child and their other Boston friends pointed out that they might be targeted for violence by Southern whites who still despised them because of their famous escape. In a letter to a friend, Child described her fears for the Crafts:

> *William and Ellen Craft are very remarkable people. With funds they have gathered in England and Boston, they are going to purchase land in their native state of Georgia, and collect a Colony of Freedmen, and establish Schools. I think they will do a great and good work, provided the devilish Ku Klux Klan does not murder them.*

Unable to talk them out of heading to the South, Child collected books for the Crafts to use in their school. Northern publishers, including the Harper Brothers, also contributed textbooks to the Crafts.

In April 1870, the Crafts left Boston and returned to Georgia. First they visited William's sister Sarah in Macon, the town the couple had fled 22 years earlier. It would be interesting to know about the reunion of the brother and sister who hadn't seen one another since being sold separately more than 30 years earlier, as well as how the ex-slaves and their former owners reacted to one another. Unfortunately, however, there is no record of the Crafts' stay in Macon.

The family then went by train to Savannah, which must have awakened memories of Ellen and William's "desperate leap for liberty." In Savannah they arranged to rent Hickory Hill, a plantation just across the Savannah River on the South Carolina side of the border with Georgia.

The Crafts cleared the fields and planted crops at Hickory Hill. While William tended the farm, Ellen began a school on their property. Assisted by her son Charles, Ellen taught the children from neighboring farms by day. At night, the mother and son opened their school to adults in the area who had never learned to read or write.

By the fall of 1870, everything was going well at Hickory Hill—*too* well, as far as some of the Crafts' white neighbors were concerned. They resented the famous ex-slaves who spoke and acted like English people. They were jealous of William for his success at farming, and of Ellen for offering black people a better education than most of them had received. Mobs of bigots gathered and vowed to teach the "uppity niggers" a lesson.

On an autumn night in 1870, men with torches set the house, barn, and school at Hickory Hill ablaze. Ellen and William awoke to the smell of smoke and the sound of men shouting. Through their windows they could see a mob of masked Ku Klux Klansmen running away. The couple led their family to safety, but much of their life savings went up in smoke.

They were tempted to give up and move back north, but Ellen and William decided that they weren't going to let a bunch of ruffians drive them away. The family moved into Savannah, where they operated a hotel while saving money for a new farm.

After about a year in Savannah they were ready to start over. They rented an abandoned farm called Woodville, located 20 miles south of Savannah in Georgia's Bryan County. The farm covered 1,800 acres or about three square miles, but it was in poor condition, with weeds in the fields, broken fences, and a house that was falling apart at the seams. Following a visit to

A black family's home set ablaze during a 1949 Ku Klux Klan reign of terror in Florida; 79 years earlier, Klansmen burned the Crafts' home.

the property, Ellen called it "a miserable hole, dirty, and full of rats and snakes all over the house." The good part was that the Crafts were able to rent Woodville for only $300 a year.

Ellen and William worked out a plan. They would invite poor black families in the area to move to Woodville. These families would help the Crafts restore and run the farm. Profits from the crops would be shared by all. Ellen would run a school on the property modeled after Ockham School in England. Along with reading and writing, the Crafts' school would provide training in carpentry, sewing, and farming so that the tenants could eventually move away and succeed on their own.

The venture began in 1872 when four families moved to Woodville. The Crafts and their tenants repaired fences, built cabins, cleared fields, and planted crops. With her children's help, Ellen transformed the main farmhouse into a decent home for her family. Soon after arriving at Woodville, Ellen Craft began teaching classes in her dining room. About 20 students of all ages, most of them tenants at Woodville, enrolled at the Woodville Cooperative Farm School, which most people simply called "Mrs. Craft's School." It began with a faculty of two: Mrs. Craft and her 11-year-old daughter and namesake, Ellen.

Maintaining the farm and school was a tremendous struggle. Money was the biggest problem. Their first year's expenses were nearly $2,000. In the fall of 1872 they sold their farm goods for only about $100. The bottom line showed a $1,900 loss. Obviously, they couldn't continue like that.

Yet they managed to survive. William returned to Massachusetts and spent about a year raising money for his wife's school by lecturing and talking to his old abolitionist friends. In her husband's absence, Ellen invited new families to Woodville, bought oxen to help with the plowing, and harvested a large crop of cotton, rice, peas, and corn. Ellen sold most of that crop in Savannah. She packed some of the vegetables into baskets, and, traveling about in her mule-drawn buggy, sold and traded them to neighbors. By the time her baskets were empty she had earned a few dollars for her school and had obtained milk and other items needed at Woodville.

William returned home with enough money to buy the farm. Once Woodville was theirs, Ellen decided that her school should have its own separate building. Her students helped her clear out an old barn and turn it into a schoolhouse. Farmers for miles around heard that Mrs. Craft's was the best school in Georgia's Bryan County (and the *only* one open to African Americans). Soon it was overflowing with students, some of whom walked ten miles to get there. From 9 A.M. until 3 P.M., the two Ellens taught dozens of children. The adults arrived at Mrs. Craft's School after sunset.

Besides teaching them reading, writing, and industrial skills, Ellen was determined to make another important change in her students' lives. Many

❧❊❧

From 9 A.M. until 3 P.M.,
the two Ellens taught dozens of children.
The adults arrived at
Mrs. Craft's School after sunset.

❧❊❧

of the parents corrected their children by whipping them, which Ellen detested. Whenever she noticed that parents were angry, she would take them out to an old graveyard on the grounds at Woodville. There she would pray with them and explain that whipping was a holdover from slavery days, when they had been the victims of it. "I have succeeded in breaking up the habit of whipping the children," Ellen proudly reported.

By the mid-1870s the barn could no longer hold all the students who wanted to attend Mrs. Craft's School. Ellen and William organized their tenants into a construction crew and built what was said to be one of Georgia's finest school buildings. Brougham, who had arrived from England, helped the two Ellens with the teaching, and Charles also seems to have pitched in at times.

Although building the school left the Crafts $2,500 in debt, they were very proud of their achievements. On July 30, 1875, a letter from William Craft appeared in the Boston *Daily Advertiser*. Sixteen families lived on the property by then, William explained. They grew cotton, rice, and corn, paying a small portion of their crops as rent. As for the Crafts' pride and joy:

Our schoolhouse is a frame building 30 by 40 [feet], one-and-a-half story, with four dormer windows. In the lower room there are three doors, and eight glass windows with outside shutters. The whole house being whitewashed, looks well for one of its kind. It stands about 300 yards from the railroad leading from Savannah to Florida. Altogether the school is highly appreciated by the colored people. There are 75 boys and girls, most of whom attend regularly. Thirty pupils reside here. The others come from the neighborhood free.

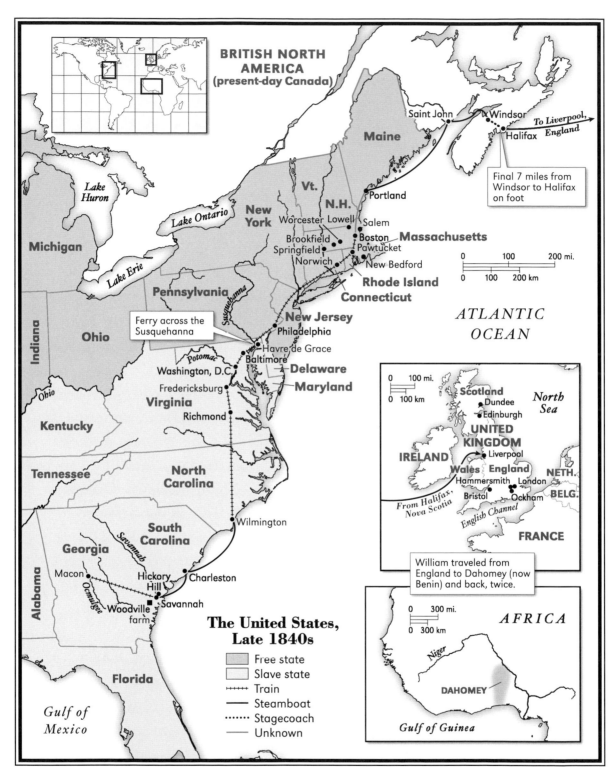

Map labels:

BRITISH NORTH AMERICA (present-day Canada)

Maine

Saint John · Windsor · Halifax — *To Liverpool, England*

Final 7 miles from Windsor to Halifax on foot

Lake Huron

Lake Ontario

Vt.

N.H.

Portland

New York

Worcester · Lowell · Salem

Brookfield · Boston · **Massachusetts**

Springfield · Pawtucket

Norwich · New Bedford

Michigan

Lake Erie

Pennsylvania

Susquehanna

Rhode Island

Connecticut

New Jersey

ATLANTIC OCEAN

Ferry across the Susquehanna

Philadelphia

Indiana

Ohio

Potomac

Havre de Grace

Baltimore

Washington, D.C.

Delaware

Maryland

Fredericksburg

Virginia

Ohio

Richmond

Kentucky

Tennessee

North Carolina

South Carolina

Georgia

Wilmington

Savannah

Macon · Hickory Hill · Charleston

Alabama

Ocmulgee

Woodville farm · Savannah

The United States, Late 1840s

- Free state
- Slave state
- Train
- Steamboat
- Stagecoach
- Unknown

Florida

Gulf of Mexico

Scale: 0 — 100 — 200 mi. / 0 — 100 — 200 km

Inset (United Kingdom):
0 — 100 mi. / 0 — 100 km
Scotland — Dundee · Edinburgh
North Sea
UNITED KINGDOM
IRELAND
Liverpool
Wales · **England** · **NETH.**
Hammersmith · London · **BELG.**
Bristol · Ockham
From Halifax, Nova Scotia
English Channel
FRANCE

William traveled from England to Dahomey (now Benin) and back, twice.

Inset (Africa):
0 — 300 mi. / 0 — 300 km
AFRICA
Niger
DAHOMEY
Gulf of Guinea

This map shows all of the places the Crafts lived and traveled in the course of their remarkable lives.

Eighteen months ago only eight or ten of the children that now attend the school knew the alphabet, but now most of them can read and write quite intelligibly....Nearly without compensation, my wife and sons have worked very hard to get the children on.

There were probably as many adults at the night school as there were children at the day school, making a total of about 150 pupils. On Sundays, the schoolhouse was transformed into a church where traveling ministers preached and Ellen taught a Sunday School class.

In their later years, Ellen and William Craft became known for their kind deeds. When neighboring families were ill, Ellen and William brought them medicine. When poor young couples needed money to get married, the Crafts helped pay for their weddings. They also took in an elderly ex-slave woman and cared for her until her death.

As the years passed, William made periodic trips north to raise funds for his wife's school. But the old-time abolitionists were dying out and the new generation had interests other than helping the ex-slaves. With not enough funds to continue, Mrs. Craft's School closed around 1880. By then Ellen and her children had taught hundreds of people to read and write.

William and Ellen Craft continued to farm at Woodville until around 1890, when he was about 67 and she about 64 years old. They then sold Woodville and retired to Charleston, South Carolina, where their children Ellen and Charles lived. They moved in with their daughter, Ellen Craft Crum, a civil rights leader who would later help found the National Federation of Afro-American Women, an organization that fought for the rights of black Americans.

Ellen and William spent their last years surrounded by their children and grandchildren. Like other grandparents, the Crafts told their grandchildren bedtime stories. Only instead of fairy tales, they told them how, a long time before, they had made a five-thousand-mile journey to freedom.

I have eight great-grandchildren,
and I tell Ellen and William's
story to each of them
when I think they're ready to hear it —
when they're between 7 and 11 years old."

Mrs. Virginia Craft Rose, great-granddaughter of Ellen and William Craft

For a quarter of a century, between 1849 and the 1870s, the Crafts were among the most famous of the tens of thousands of escaped slaves. Many articles and books kept their story in the public eye. In William Wells Brown's *Three Years in Europe*, published in London in 1852, he told of his travels with William and Ellen. Brown's novel *Clotel; or, The President's Daughter* featured characters modeled after the Georgia Fugitives. William and Ellen's *Running a Thousand Miles for Freedom* was the first book to contain details about their escape. Five years later, in 1865, newly freed slaves were introduced to the Crafts through *The Freedmen's Book* by Lydia Maria Child.

William Still had compiled notes on the Crafts, as well as on hundreds of other escaped slaves whom he had helped. If seized by slave catchers, he realized, his papers could be used to recapture the fugitives, so Still stored his notes in a secret place: the loft of a building in a Philadelphia cemetery. At the end of the Civil War, he retrieved his records from their hiding place and used them to write *The Underground Railroad*, which introduced the Crafts to a new generation of readers.

Yet by the time they had closed Mrs. Craft's School around 1880, Ellen and William had faded into obscurity. Some basic facts about their last years remain uncertain, including the dates of their deaths. At least one book claims

Two girls present flowers to Virginia Craft Rose (left) *and her British cousin, Hilda Nicholson, in Hammersmith, England. Hilda is the grand-daughter of Ellen and William's third son, Brougham.*

that Ellen died in the early 1890s. However, Emily DeCosta, the wife of Ellen and William's great-grandson Herbert, says that date is wrong.

"I read in books that Ellen died in 1891," Mrs. DeCosta told us. "But according to family records, Ellen died in 1897, and William died three years after her in 1900. There's an old family story that Ellen was buried under her favorite tree at Woodville. My husband Herbert and I went there but we didn't find anything. Currently, the location is an upscale housing development."

The Crafts and their story remained largely forgotten for nearly a century. The civil rights movement of the 1960s revived interest in black heroes and heroines of the past. William and Ellen's book, *Running a Thousand Miles for Freedom,* was reissued in 1969. Two years later, Florence Freedman's children's book, *Two Tickets to Freedom: The True Story of Ellen and William Craft, Fugitive Slaves,* was published. The following year a documentary film based on the Crafts' escape, *A Slave's Story: Running a Thousand Miles to Freedom,* was released. Historian Dorothy Sterling devoted a third of her 1979 book, *Black Foremothers: Three Lives,* to the Crafts.

But all along, there was one group of people for whom the Georgia Fugitives were very much alive. For six generations, the story of their courageous escape has been handed down by the Craft family. As of 2006, Ellen and William had numerous descendants in the United States and England. Most of those we spoke with had heard their ancestors' story when young.

"I was in high school when I first heard about my great-grandparents," recalled 80-year-old Mrs. Bernice Craft DeCosta Davis. The granddaughter of the Crafts' firstborn child, Charles Estlin Phillips Craft, Bernice peppered her relatives with questions about Ellen and William and read everything she could find about them.

"I was very proud of their accomplishments," continued Mrs. Davis. "Later I told my own two daughters the story, and they also read about it. I think when children see what people have gone through for the sake of freedom it gives them something to think about."

One person we spoke to explained that her thoughts often turn to the Crafts in daily life. "They left us a tremendous legacy to live up to," said Gail DeCosta, their great-great-granddaughter. "I hope I'm living a life that Ellen and William would be proud of. It's important to hand down this story because the generations today are failing to know what we have gone through. They don't know much about slavery and the civil rights movement and are losing what we fought so hard to get. I told my own daughter, Julia, who is now in her twenties, about the Crafts when she was a child."

"My mother had a picture of Ellen on her mantle," says Gail's daughter, Julia DeCosta Hodges, "and my grandparents, Herbert and Emily DeCosta, had pictures of Ellen and William in their bedroom. As a child, I thought their story was pretty neat, and the fact that I was related to them just made it more interesting. I appreciate it

Shane Aldridge portraying his great-great-great-great-grandmother Ellen for his class.

more now. Their story gives me a greater sense of purpose and family pride.

"There's a lot that can be gained from their story. First, it shows what enslaved Africans went through and how important it is to have basic freedom. It's also important to see how determination can carry people through a very difficult task."

Today a new generation of Craft descendants is helping to keep Ellen and William's remarkable story alive. Ten-year-old Shane Aldridge is the Crafts' great-great-great-great-grandson. "Every year during Black History Month I do an oral report about the Crafts," Shane told us. "Other children should know about Ellen and William because their story shows how thinking and planning can make your life happier even when it seems impossible.

"One day I will tell my children and grandchildren about Ellen and William Craft so that they will know about their ancestors and fight for what is right like they did."

1823	William Craft is born in Georgia
1826	Ellen Smith is born in Clinton, Georgia
1834	Slavery is outlawed in the British Empire, including Canada
1837	Ellen moves to Macon, Georgia, as her half-sister's slave
1839	William and his sister Sarah are sold; he becomes slave of Mr. Ira Taylor of Macon
1844	Ellen and William meet at about this time
1846	Ellen and William have a slave wedding
1848	December 21, Ellen and William Craft make a daring break for freedom
	December 25, Crafts reach freedom in Philadelphia, Pennsylvania
1849	January 1, Crafts hide at Ivens farm outside Philadelphia
	Mid-January, Crafts depart for Boston, Massachusetts
	January–May, the Georgia Fugitives tour New England with William Wells Brown
	May, Crafts settle at Hayden home in Boston
1850	September 18, Fugitive Slave Law takes effect
	October 21, Slave catchers Knight and Hughes arrive in Boston
	November 7, Reverend Theodore Parker performs wedding ceremony for Crafts
	December, Crafts arrive in Liverpool, England
1851	Crafts make a lecture tour of Britain and enroll at Ockham School
1852	October 22, Charles, the Crafts' first child, is born
1853	Crafts move to London
1855	William Craft Jr. is born
1857	Son Brougham is born
1860	*Running a Thousand Miles for Freedom* is published
1861	Civil War begins; daughter Ellen is born
1862	William's first trip to Africa
1864	William's second trip to Africa
1865	Civil War ends, freeing the slaves; Ellen's mother arrives in England
1869	Ellen and William's youngest child, Alfred, is born; family returns to Boston
1870	Crafts return to Georgia; rent Hickory Hill plantation in South Carolina, which is burned by the Ku Klux Klan
1872	Mrs. Craft's School opens in Bryan County, Georgia
1880	Mrs. Craft's School closes around this time
1890	Ellen and William retire to Charleston, South Carolina, around this time
1897	Ellen Craft dies at the age of 71
1900	William Craft dies in January at age 76

NOTES

Ellen Craft and William Craft are abbreviated as EC and WC. The Crafts' book *Running a Thousand Miles for Freedom* is abbreviated as *Running*.

Chapter 1: A DESPERATE LEAP FOR LIBERTY

pp. 6–9 The Crafts described their departure and what they said to each other on pp. 35–42 of *Running*.

p. 7 The torture known as the "picket" is described on p. 37 of *From Slavery to Agrarian Capitalism in the Cotton Plantation South: Central Georgia, 1800–1880* by Joseph R. Reidy.

Chapter 2: YEARS IN BONDAGE

p. 11 Information about the Georgia Central Railroad comes from p. 74 of *From Slavery to Agrarian Capitalism* by Reidy.

p. 12 The Bibb County population figures come from the appendix of Reidy's book.

p. 14 The 1835 threatened slave revolt in Georgia's Monroe County is described by Reidy on pp. 28–29.

pp. 16–18 and pp. 20–21 EC's early life is described on pp. 5–10 of *Black Foremothers: Three Lives* by Dorothy Sterling.

pp. 18–20 WC's early life is described on pp. 9–13 of *Running*.

pp. 22–24 The Crafts' plans for their escape and their conversations about it are described on pp. 27–35 of *Running*; additional information comes from *The Black Abolitionist Papers*, edited by Peter C. Ripley, volume 1, pp. 246–249.

Chapter 3: THE FIRST THOUSAND MILES

pp. 25–39 All of the events and conversations regarding the escape to Philadelphia come from pp. 43–79 of *Running*.

Chapter 4: THE CITY OF BROTHERLY LOVE

pp. 41–45 Most of the events and all of the dialogue for this chapter were found in pp. 80–86 of *Running*.

p. 42 William Still's description of the impression EC made upon him appears on p. 370 of his book *The Underground Railroad*.

pp. 42–45 Information about William Wells Brown comes from *Narrative of William Wells Brown, A Fugitive Slave*.

pp. 43 William Wells Brown's article in the January 12, 1849, *Liberator* is reprinted on pp. 22–23 of *Black Foremothers: Three Lives* by Dorothy Sterling.

Chapter 5: THE CRADLE OF LIBERTY

p. 47 The Wendell Phillips quotes appear on p. 23 of *Black Foremothers: Three Lives* by Dorothy Sterling.

pp. 47-48 The Crafts' tour with William Wells Brown is described on pp. 23–25 of *Black Foremothers*.

p. 48–49 The "Runaway Slaves" article appeared in the February 13, 1849, *Georgia Telegraph*.

pp. 50–57 The incidents and dialogue concerning the slave catchers Isaac Scott, John Knight, and Willis Hughes come from pp. 88–91 of *Running*; from pp. 28–33 of *Black Foremothers*; and from pp. 95–100 of volume 2 of *Life and Correspondence of Theodore Parker* by John Weiss.

p. 51 Section 7 of the Fugitive Slave Law appears on p. 87 of *The Negro Almanac*.

p. 54 Willis Hughes's "I am the jailer at Macon" quote appeared in the November 5, 1850, Milledgeville *Federal Union*.

p. 55 Willis Hughes's assertion that he was arrested in the Boston area "for smoking in the streets" and other offenses appears in the November 26, 1850, Milledgeville *Federal Union*.

p. 57 Willis Hughes's statement about "the abolition sentiment in Boston" also comes from the November 26, 1850, Milledgeville *Federal Union*.

p. 57–58 President Millard Fillmore's response through an aide appears in the *Georgia Citizen* of Macon of November 14, 1850.

p. 58 Reverend Theodore Parker's November 6, 1850, journal entry, "Ellen Craft has been here all the week," comes from p. 99 of volume 2 of *Life and Correspondence* by Weiss.

pp. 59 The wedding Reverend Parker performed for EC and WC is described on pp. 99–100 of volume 2 of *Life and Correspondence* by Weiss.

Chapter 6: FUGITIVES AGAIN

pp. 61–63 The events and conversations that occurred during the Crafts' flight from Boston to Liverpool are described on pp. 100–108 of *Running*.

Chapter 7: A NEW LIFE IN ENGLAND

pp. 65–77 Much of the information about the Crafts' life in England comes from volume 1 of *The Black Abolitionist Papers* and from pp. 37–49 of *Black Foremothers: Three Lives* by Dorothy Sterling.

p. 68 William Still's December 30, 1850 speech in Edinburgh comes from pp. 246–249 of volume 1 of *The Black Abolitionist Papers*.

pp. 71 EC's letter asserting that she wouldn't "be a slave for the best man that ever breathed upon the American continent" appears on pp. 330–331 of volume I of *The Black Abolitionist Papers*.

pp. 73–75 Information about WC's trips to Africa was found on pp. 199–202 of *The Freedmen's Book* by Lydia Maria Child.

p. 73 WC told about his grandparents coming from West Africa in a talk he made in England which is recorded in *The Black Abolitionist Papers,* volume 1, p. 541.

Chapter 8: GOING HOME

pp. 79–87 Much of the information for this chapter comes from pp. 49–59 of *Black Foremothers* by

Sterling, and from Florence B. Freedman's introduction to *Running,* pp. xv–xix.

pp. 81 Lydia Maria Child's letter about the Crafts appears on p. 50 of *Black Foremothers: Three Lives.*

pp. 86 WC's letter about their schoolhouse appears on pp. xvii–xviii of Freedman's introduction to *Running.*

AFTERWORD

p. 89-91 Emily DeCosta, Mrs. Bernice Craft DeCosta Davis, Gail DeCosta, Julia DeCosta Hodges, and Shane Aldridge told us about their ancestors, EC and WC, in 2004.

BIBLIOGRAPHY

BOOKS

Brown, John. *Slave Life in Georgia.* London: Chamerovzow, 1855 (reprinted 1971).

Chadwick, John White. *Theodore Parker: Preacher and Reformer.* Boston: Houghton, Mifflin, 1900.

Child, Lydia Maria. *The Freedmen's Book.* Boston: Ticknor and Fields, 1865 (reprinted 1968).

Commager, Henry Steele. *Theodore Parker.* Boston: Little, Brown, 1936.

Craft, William, and Ellen Craft. *Running a Thousand Miles for Freedom; or, the Escape of William and Ellen Craft from Slavery.* London: Tweedie, 1860 (reprinted 1969).

Freedman, Florence B. *Two Tickets to Freedom: The True Story of Ellen and William Craft, Fugitive Slaves.* New York: Simon and Schuster, 1971.

Jefferson, Paul, ed. *The Travels of William Wells Brown* (includes reprint of 1847 edition of *Narrative of William Wells Brown, A Fugitive Slave).* Edinburgh, Scotland: Edinburgh University Press, 1991.

Ploski, Harry A., and Roscoe C. Brown Jr., eds. *The Negro Almanac.* New York: Bellwether, 1967.

Reidy, Joseph P. *From Slavery to Agrarian Capitalism in the Cotton Plantation South: Central Georgia, 1800–1880.* Chapel Hill: University of North Carolina Press, 1992.

Ripley, C. Peter, ed. *The Black Abolitionist Papers* (5 volumes). Chapel Hill: University of North Carolina Press, 1985–1992.

Sterling, Dorothy. *Black Foremothers: Three Lives* (2nd edition). New York: Feminist Press, 1988.

Still, William. *The Underground Railroad.* Philadelphia: Porter & Coates, 1872.

Weiss, John. *Life and Correspondence of Theodore Parker* (2 volumes). New York: Appleton, 1864 (reprinted 1969).

NEWSPAPERS

Federal Union (of Milledgeville, Georgia): November 5, November 26, December 3, 1850.

Georgia Citizen (of Macon): November 2, November 14, 1850.

Georgia Journal and Messenger (of Macon): November 6, November 13, November 20, December 4, 1850; June 25, 1851.

Georgia Telegraph (of Macon): February 13, 1849; November 19, 1850.

Macon Telegraph and Messenger: June 12, 1878.

New York Herald: November 20, 1850.

VIDEO

A Slave's Story: Running a Thousand Miles to Freedom. Learning Corporation of America, 1972. Copies of the video can be obtained from Coronet/MTI Film and Video, a division of the Phoenix Learning Group, Inc., 2349 Chaffee Drive, St. Louis, MO 63146. (314) 569-0211 or (800) 221-1274.

INTERVIEWS BY THE AUTHORS

(All took place in 2004)
Noah Aldridge
Shane Aldridge
Skylar Aldridge
Bernice Craft DeCosta Davis
Emily DeCosta
Gail DeCosta
Julia DeCosta Hodges
Virginia Craft Rose